Assistive Technology:

An Introductory Guide for K–12 Library Media Specialists

by **Janet Hopkins**
with a chapter by **JP Schnapper-Casteras**

Your Trusted
Library-to-Classroom Connection.
Books, Magazines, and Online

Library of Congress Cataloging-in-Publication Data

Hopkins, Janet.
  Assistive technology : an introductory guide for K-12 library media specialists / by Janet
Hopkins; with a chapter by J.P. Schnapper-Casteras.
    p. cm.
Includes bibliographical references (p.) and index.
  ISBN 1-58683-138-0 (pbk)
  1. School libraries–Services to people with disabilities–United States. 2. Children with
disabilities–Services for–United States. 3. Youth with disabilities–Services for–United States. 4.
Libraries and children with disabilities–United States. 5. Assistive computer technology–United
States. 6. Self-help devices for people with disabilities–United States. I. Title.
Z711.92.H3H67 2004
027.6'63–dc22

                                2004000661

Publishing by Linworth Publishing, Inc.
480 East Wilson Bridge Road, Suite L
Worthington, OH 43085

ISBN: 1-58683-138-0

5 4 3 2 1

▶ Table **of Contents**

Table of Figures

▶ Acknowledgments

The idea of writing a book about assistive technology (AT) for library media specialists was suggested to me after Linworth Publishing's Editorial Director Carol Simpson invited me to submit a magazine article about AT to *Library Media Connection* (LMC). Linworth's interest in this topic provided the motivation I needed to organize my ideas for the book. This writing opportunity came at a perfect time, as I had taken a leave from my regular teaching assignment and had more flexibility and time to devote to this project.

I have been fortunate to work under the editorial guidance of Judi Repman and Donna Miller. Their experience helped me to enjoy my authoring/telecommuting adventure, as they provided prompt responses to my questions and reliable support throughout the writing process. In addition to the important encouragement of Linworth Publishing, I have been assisted by my enormously supportive family and interested contributors.

A book about assistive technology would not be possible without the visionary and talented developers who have responded to the needs of people with disabilities. I am continuously impressed by the contributions of many individuals, companies, and organizations that have created so many amazing AT solutions. These efforts range from individuals who volunteer their time to corporate high-tech teams. All of these developers are doing important work, and their skills are very much appreciated.

I am also thankful to many professionals and consumers with AT experience who share their knowledge about enabling technology in many ways. These are individuals who participate on Internet discussion groups, write articles and books, construct Web resources, organize conferences and courses, and give presentations. This book contains much information that has been gained over the years from people who have generously contributed in these ways and others. I would especially like to thank individuals who have shared their expertise in this book through chapter and sidebar content: Scott Bellman, Gayl Bowser, Sheryl Burgstahler, Alison Linganc, Janet Murray, Penny Reed, and JP Schnapper-Casteras.

▶ Product and Company Acknowledgments

Numerous products and company names are mentioned throughout this book. Various copyrights, trademarks, and service marks included in this book are the copyrights, trademarks, and service marks of their respective owners.

▶ **About** the **Author**

Janet Hopkins has worked as a secondary school teacher in central British Columbia, Canada, since 1981. She has taught in both general and special education classrooms and is a RESNA (Rehabilitation Engineering and Assistive Technology Society of North America) Certified Assistive Technology Practitioner. She works as a consultant and freelance writer through her business, Assistive Tech Educational Consulting. Hopkins is the founder and moderator of the Assistive Technology Canada Listserv, an online discussion group to support educators and members of the public who have an interest in special needs technology. Hopkins is co-maintainer of the Linux Accessibility Resource Site and writes and publishes "Special Needs Tech News," a free quarterly e-newsletter. Hopkins has written articles about assistive technology for *ComputorEdge*, *Closing the Gap*, *Inclusion Times*, *AbilityHub*, *Canadian Disability Magazine*, *Diabetes Self-Management Magazine*, *Library Media Connection*, *YES Magazine*, and other publications. Hopkins was the first Canadian recipient of the Curriculum Associates, Inc., "Excellence in Teaching Cabinet Grant" and has done writing work for the National School Boards Association. Hopkins lives with her husband and three children in Kamloops, British Columbia. More information about her work is available on her Web site <http://ca.geocities.com/janethopkinsbc>. Hopkins can be contacted by e-mail at <AT_Consulting@Canada.com>.

▶ **Contributing Author**

JP Schnapper-Casteras is a student at Stanford University (Class of 2005). He is the organizer of the 1st, 2nd, and 3rd Linux Accessibility Conferences and the coordinator of the Free Desktop Accessibility Working Group (FDAWG). JP is the creator and maintainer of the Linux Accessibility Resource Site (LARS) and the founder and former maintainer of the KDE Accessibility Project. He is a consultant for the Trace Research and Development Center at the University of Wisconsin, Madison. He has written several articles and papers on the subject of Linux accessibility.

Within the discipline of Computer Science, he is interested in accessibility, usability, post-desktop interfaces, universal design, and Human Computer Interaction. JP also has a strong interest in political science and economics. In his free time, he enjoys composing jazz, blues, and other styles of music for the piano, photography, dancing, and spending time with awesome friends and family. JP can be reached by e-mail at <jpsc@stanford.edu>.

▶ Introduction

If you are not already aware of the term assistive technology (AT), it may sound unfamiliar and intimidating. AT is a relatively new and rapidly emerging field. It is a technology sub-specialty that is usually associated with professionals working in the fields of special education and rehabilitation. Like most educators, you have probably not received pre-service training, methodology, or professional development related to AT.

Increasingly, educators are learning about the educational role of assistive technology and its potential to bolster student achievement. It is true that many professionals now working in the field of assistive technology have devoted a great deal of their personal time to learn about AT. Why did they do it? Why do they continue to do it?

I cannot speak for all of the educational AT enthusiasts on the planet, but I have my own reasons for wanting to submerge myself in the field. In 1997, I was assigned to a new position as the severe learning disabilities teacher at a mid-sized high school. Partly because I had brand new computer equipment arrive that year and partly because I felt poorly equipped for the assignment, I started to research technology options for my students who had severe learning disabilities.

I became familiar with the Internet and taught myself how to surf the Web. I stumbled across the term "assistive technology" while visiting a Web site about learning disabilities. That single resource led me to many other online AT resources. I became fascinated and wanted to learn more.

My search for AT solutions led to the classroom implementation of some innovative products I had discovered through my cyber travels. It was incredibly rewarding to find, investigate, and evaluate new products and to see how they could help my students. It was just as exciting for the students who thrived on AT as it was for me. We shared the adventure and the enthusiasm for new technologies and this helped them to demonstrate their knowledge and learn more independently. Introducing my students to assistive technology made me feel more useful as a teacher than I had ever felt in my career.

It is not necessary for all educators to have an in-depth knowledge of AT to be effective in their jobs. However, it is necessary for some educators to gain knowledge about the field of assistive technology. Educators who interact with special needs students and their parents need to have knowledge about AT. Parents, who are strong advocates for their children, are becoming informed about assistive technology and expect educators to have knowledge and experience with AT.

Inclusive schools are the norm across most of the western world. Parents want their children with disabilities to have opportunities to learn and participate along side their able-bodied peers. As the K–12 library media center is the central learning resource in most schools, it is incumbent upon administrators and library media specialists to provide accessible facilities and resources.

This book is a guide that will assist K–12 library media specialists and others who are unfamiliar with assistive technology or have limited knowledge about AT. The book presents topics related to inclusion and accessibility, information about categories of assistive technology, and online resources that will help readers to extend their knowledge through independent Internet research.

Chapters 1 through 5 include discussion of the library media center's role within the inclusive school setting, as it relates to both students and staff. The concept of universal design for learning is reviewed along with relevant legislation and school reform initiatives. The role of assistive technology, AT teams, assessment, and funding considerations are also addressed. Technology options, categories, accessibility needs, and initiatives are covered in Chapters 6 through 14. The final chapter provides information related to professional development opportunities and online opportunities that provide collegial support.

The book contains a combination of factual information and opinions, based on the experiences and expertise of people who have contributed information through interviews and sidebar submissions, as well as an entire chapter—Chapter 9 (Linux/Open Source), written by JP Schnapper-Casteras. These generous and experienced contributors have helped me to present a "conference within a book." The table of contents and index are quick reference tools that allow the reader to scan the book for information on specific topics. However, it is recommended that the book be read from start to finish, as the concepts and technologies discussed early on provide a foundation for understanding the content in subsequent chapters.

It is important to mention that it is not possible for the visual content of a book of this length to provide a complete review of all of the AT-related products, Web sites, and resources that exist. Readers should understand that the products that have been mentioned or selected as visual examples are often not the only available products of their kind. Readers are encouraged to investigate numerous product options before making a selection or purchasing decision. There are re-sellers, developers, and helpful online searchable databases in addition to those mentioned in the book that can help readers learn about a wider range of products and resources. The products that are pictured or discussed in this book are included as examples and represent the wide range of technologies and resources available. While these products may be appropriate options for some consumers, it is not suggested that they will meet the needs of all consumers.

You will not learn everything about assistive technology by reading this book. As innovative technologies are continuously being developed, it is impossible for any one person to know it all in this field. However, this book provides an orientation that can reduce the time required to gain a basic level of understanding about this field. Unfortunately, this book cannot provide hands-on experience with assistive technology, but information about conferences and software download links, which can help you gain that experience, are listed.

This book is shaped through my own interest in assistive technology, as well as the valuable contributions, expertise, and collective knowledge of many people and organizations. It will guide you on your AT journey and help you make connections that will allow you to continue to learn about assistive technology.

Chapter 1

Inclusive K-12 Education and Library Services

Many special educators are expanding their knowledge about the field of assistive technology. Assistive technology (AT) can help improve access to print and electronic text resources for individuals with disabilities. AT can also help to minimize other barriers to learning and using a computer. As library media centers are the schools' centralized information and learning resources, it is important for library media specialists to become aware of the value of AT. Students with disabilities require specialized support to access library materials and computer technology. Library media specialists must establish partnerships with special educators as well as general educators to ensure that special needs students receive appropriate library services and access to assistive technology.

Over the last 10 to 20 years, considerable changes have taken place in North American education systems with respect to the provision of services for students with disabilities. Education systems have been successful in expanding the range of K–12 programming available to students. The "one size fits all" style of teaching has been gradually shifting toward instructional methods that recognize the existence of multiple learning styles. Educators are becoming more aware of the increasingly diverse characteristics of students within the education system. Classroom teachers and library media specialists are continuously evaluating the needs of their students and reinventing their instructional materials, settings, delivery, and strategies to engage all learners.

Although this book is intended to provide helpful information to library media specialists and educators across North America and beyond, this guide primarily makes reference to U.S.-based resources. These are provided to create awareness about some of the attitudinal, policy, health, and demographic influences on education. Currently, there are more educational assistive technology (AT) initiatives and extensive legislation regarding educational AT entitlement in the United States than in other countries.

The School Library

The library media center functions as a meeting place for the school community. Frequently used for staff meetings, parent/teacher gatherings, and hosting guest speakers, it is difficult to imagine another location in the school with the potential to play such a versatile role.

Although the library media center has an important social function for students and staff, its primary purpose is to facilitate independent learning, research, and study skills. This can be achieved by making resources available to support the efficient and effective use of materials by students and staff and to meet the curriculum standards and recreational needs of the school community.

The Hub of the Inclusive School Community

The library media center has the potential to be the hub of the inclusive school. However, it takes adequate funding and staffing to accomplish this. Resources that cover academic, reference, and recreational reading topics will encourage students and staff from all grades and departments to make use of library facilities. The well-equipped library media center becomes a magnet for learning and productive social interaction. Library media centers that have been neglected or understaffed in relation to school enrollment are less able to meet the needs of the entire school community. In a well-funded program, students and staff use the library media center during class time, lunch breaks, and before and after school. As long as the library media center doors are open, opportunities for individual and collaborative learning are available.

Well-staffed and equipped library media centers have been shown to have a positive influence on student academic performance. A 1994 study of schools in Colorado, Pennsylvania, and Alaska concluded that "students at schools with better-funded Library media centers tend to achieve higher average reading scores, whether their schools and communities are rich or poor and whether adults in their community are well or poorly educated" (Lance, K. Curry, 1994). The study released by the Colorado State Library's Library Research Service and the University of Denver's Library and Information Services Department also concluded that library funding is important for providing adequate levels of staffing and a large collection of materials in a variety of formats.

Direct U.S. federal funding for school libraries was eliminated over 20 years ago; thus, it is now crucial for school boards and administrators in the United States to understand the important role library media centers play in supporting student achievement. As part of the Bush administration's No Child Left Behind legislation, signed into law in January 2002, there has been some recognition of the need for increased library media center funding.

Shaping the Future

In low-income neighborhoods, the school library media center may be one of the few learning resources available to enrich children's lives. On average, children who come from poor families have less exposure to reading materials before starting school than children who come from higher-income households. It is to be expected that these poorer students also have less technology available to them at home.

The emergence of a growing digital divide between affluent and poor populations should be of concern to educators and policy makers. Creating equitable access to information needs to be a priority for educational jurisdictions everywhere.

Fortunately, there have been some positive developments over the last eight years as more school computers have become connected to the Internet. The growing emphasis on technology spending has concerned some educators who worry other educational priorities may not be addressed. As long as schools make the effort to achieve a balance between traditional library and classroom materials and high-tech resources, students and staff will be well served. Internet resources complement print and multimedia materials by expanding access to up-to-date sources of information. Computers also provide new opportunities for helping students with disabilities achieve greater independence.

The National Education Association (NEA) in the United States supports federal programs to help schools buy computer technology and to upgrade classroom technology. However, the NEA believes that the provision of hardware and software alone is not the complete solution to creating better schools.

> *In order to prepare students to put this vast "sea of information" to good use, teachers, paraprofessionals, library media specialists and other school technology professionals themselves must have quality professional development and ongoing technical assistance. Technology's ability to transcend time and geographical limitations opens vast new opportunities. However, it's important to recognize that teaching in a new format requires vastly different skills, approaches and support*

*systems (**Technology**, National Education Association, September 10, 2002).*

The number of connected classrooms and library media centers will continue to grow, but how confident do educators feel about their role in wired and wireless schools?

The School and Library Staff

Most library media specialists are capable of leading students and staff through search engine and database orientations so that able-bodied students can independently hunt for materials on a specific topic. Library media specialists as well as other educators have been able to make new technology available to staff and students, but surveys indicate that not all teachers feel prepared when it comes to teaching with technology.

Attitudes and Awareness

Just as there are learning variations among students when it comes to academic skill development, there will be variation among educators when it come to technological skill development.

Library media specialists may have better opportunities to work with students on computers on a regular basis than some of their colleagues in classrooms. Teachers who spend most of their time in classrooms without computers can't be expected to have the same grasp of hardware and software applications as their colleagues who have daily access to computers while they work. Students of teachers who have little background, time, or opportunity to learn about computers can really benefit from the technology skills and assistance of library media specialists.

Collaboration

Library media specialists are in a special position to assist classroom teachers and their students who wish to become more comfortable using technology. A team approach to the instructional use of technology helps teachers to improve their teaching skills and competency with technology by sharing knowledge.

Architects of Inclusion

Educators, parents, and students all play a role in shaping the inclusive learning environment. Everyone in the school community should be considered part of the inclusion team.

The Clients

Administrators, library media specialists, classroom teachers, and support personnel have a wide range of students to consider when planning lessons and purchasing learning materials. How will changes in student populations and enrollment influence education?

From 1998–99 to 2000, there was an increase of 2.6% in the number of students in the United States, ages six to 21, served under the Individuals with Disabilities Education Act. This increase in the number of special education students may be the result of improved identification of special needs students. However, infant birth weight trends signal an increase in the numbers of students who will require special education services in the future.

Technology has led to improved medical outcomes for high-risk and pre-term births. This may be part of the reason why the numbers of low birth weight babies is on the rise. From 1980 to 2000 in the United States, the percentage of low birth weight infants (<2500 grams) increased 11.8% and that of very low birth weight infants (<1500 grams) increased 24.3% (***Infant Mortality and Low Birth Weight Among Black and White Infants—United States, 1980–2000, Centers for Disease Control and Prevention***). According to the World Health Organization, the birth weight of an infant is the single most important determinant of its chances of survival and healthy growth and development. Low birth weight babies are at greater risk for developmental and learning disabilities.

Students and Staff with Disabilities

School personnel are working with a wider range of students who require special consideration when it comes to education. The rate of inclusion of special needs students in regular classrooms has been increasing. Educators need new resources to help them find ways of connecting with all of their students. Traditional materials and assistive technologies can be used together to provide better access to learning.

It is important that special needs students have the opportunity to socialize with other students. Special needs students need the opportunity to participate in class in a manner that is as similar to the participation of other students as possible. Special needs students should be given the tools they need to independently demonstrate their knowledge and abilities, with as little extra assistance as necessary.

Staff members with disabilities can be excellent role models for all students. Additionally, many disability advocacy groups in the community are willing to visit schools to help create awareness. Disability awareness activities can be incorporated into many subject areas to promote discussion about disability issues. Library media specialists and other staff members can share classroom strategies that help improve learning opportunities for students with special needs.

There are a number of excellent online resources that provide advice on classroom accommodations and strategies for students with special needs. The University of Toronto's SNOW (Special Needs Opportunity Windows) Web site has some helpful suggestions for teachers of special needs students. Strategies to Assist Students With Special Needs can be found at <http://snow.utoronto.ca/best/accommodate/>.

▶ References

Department of Education Taking Applications for Money to Improve School Libraries, U.S. Department of Education press release, May 30, 2002 <http://reed.senate.gov/releases/0168.htm>.

Herndon, Lucia, *The Sorry State of Philadelphia School Libraries*, Philadelphia Inquirer, October 17, 1999 <http://www.libraries.phila.k12.pa.us/newsreports/lucia-10-17-99.html>.

Inclusion of Students with Disabilities in Regular Classrooms, National Center for Education Statistics, Office of Educational Research & Improvement, U.S. Department of Education <http://nces.ed.gov//programs/coe/2002/section4/indicator28.asp>.

Infant Mortality and Low Birth Weight Among Black and White Infants—United States, 1980–2000, Morbidity and Mortality Weekly Report, July 12, 2002, Centers for Disease Control and Prevention <http://www.cdc.gov/mmwr/preview/mmwrhtml/mm5127a1.htm>.

Internet Access, National Center for Education Statistics, Office of Educational Research & Improvement, U.S. Department of Education <http://nces.ed.gov/fastfacts/display.asp?id=46>.

Lance, Keith Curry, *The Impact of School Library Media Centers on Academic Achievement*, School Library Media Research, Vol. 22 No. 3 Spring 1994, American Association of School Librarians <http://www.ala.org/aasl/SLMR/slmr_resources/select_lance.html>.

Murray, C., *Study Reveals Shifts in Digital Divide for Students*, eSchool News, March 20, 2003 <http://www.eschoolnews.com/news/showStoryalert.cfm?ArticleID=4309>.

Rowand, C., *Teacher Use of Computers and the Internet in Public Schools*, Education Statistics Quarterly, April 2000 <http://nces.ed.gov/pubs2000/quarterly/summer/3elem/q3-2.html>.

Students with Disabilities, National Center for Education Statistics, Office of Educational Research & Improvement, U.S. Department of Education <http://nces.ed.gov//programs/coe/2002/notes/n10.asp>.

Students' Use of the Internet, National Center for Education Statistics, Office of Educational Research & Improvement, U.S. Department Education <http://nces.ed.gov/programs/coe/2000/section4/indicator45.asp>.

Teachers' Readiness to Use Computers and the Internet, National Center for Education Statistics, Office of Educational Research & Improvement, U.S. Department of Education <http://nces.ed.gov/programs/coe/2001/section4/indicator39.asp>.

Technology, National Education Association, September 10, 2002 <http://www.nea.org/technology/>.

Twenty-third Annual Report to Congress on the Implementation of the Individuals with Disabilities Education Act (2001), United States Department of Education, Office of Special Education Programs <http://www.ed.gov/offices/OSERS/OSEP/Products/OSEP2001AnlRpt/index.html>.

Chapter 2

Definitions and Legal Considerations

As assistive technology (AT) covers strategies and supports that are used to help individuals with disabilities in health, rehabilitation, and education fields, there can be some overlap regarding the application of systems and devices.

Although the focus of this book is on AT for the K–12 library media center, it is useful to have a broader understanding of the field and issues related to the use and implementation of assistive technology in education. In the United States, the *Technology-Related Assistance For Individuals With Disabilities Act Of 1988 As Amended In 1994, Section 3. Definitions (Public Laws 100-407 and 103-218)* includes definitions on assistive technology that are widely quoted in publications about assisitive technology. The Tech Act definitions for assistive tcchnology dcvicc and assistivc tcchnology scrvice are available online through the Rehabilitation Engineering and Assistive Technology Society of North America (RESNA) Web page <http://www.resna.org/taproject/library/laws/techact94.htm>.

> *Assistive technology device: The term "assistive technology device" means any item, piece of equipment, or product system, whether acquired commercially off the shelf, modified, or customized, that is used to increase, maintain, or improve functional capabilities of individuals with disabilities.*

Assistive Technology

Essentially, assistive technology is a product or a service that enables independence. The term assistive technology may be new to some people, but AT has been commonly used for a long time. Eyeglasses, wheelchairs, tape recorders, and bookmarks could all come under the heading of assistive technology for persons who must use these devices to function more independently and efficiently. Assistive technology applications and products range from very simplistic to very complex.

Assistive technology can facilitate access to the curriculum and enhance participation. For example, non-verbal students are able to use augmentative communication devices, signaling, and symbol systems to communicate in a classroom setting. Students with hearing impairments may receive preferential seating and make use of assistive listening devices. Instructors who have difficulty projecting their voices in a classroom setting can reach their audiences with the use of voice amplification devices.

There are numerous classifications of assistive technology products. The field of assistive technology contains sub-specialties of AT. Because of the range of devices, and because the rate of product development and innovation is so rapid, it is impossible for any one person to know everything about assistive technology. Within the education field, AT is of interest to library media specialists, school psychologists, speech language pathologists, special educators, classroom teachers, as well as physical education instructors who provide adaptive sports equipment for special needs students. Some other professionals who work with AT include orthotists, prosthetists, physical therapists, occupational therapists, rehabilitation engineers, and audiologists.

Assistive technology products can be classified under specialty categories. Certain devices may be considered valuable for several categories of use. For example, screen-reading software can be used to meet the needs of individuals who require communication, vision, or literacy support. The product category divisions found on the *assistivetech.net* Web site provide an outline of the scope of the field of assistive technology.

The *assistivetech.net* site is sponsored by the National Institute on Disability and Rehabilitation Research and the Georgia Tech Center

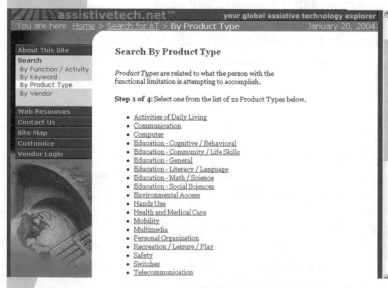

Figure 2.1: assistivetech.net Product Search Page
<http://www.assistivetech.net/search/product_type_search.cfm>
[Reprinted with permission from the Georgia Tech Research Corporation.]

for Assistive Technology and Environmental Access. It provides a searchable database of products that conform to these categories. Search options at this site include Function/Activity Search, Keyword Search, Product Type Search, and Vendor Search. Other organizations that provide assistive technology information online may classify AT according to different headings. Assistive technology products and strategies may be low tech (raised line writing paper), mid tech (tape recorder), or high tech (word processing software).

Low Tech

Because low-tech AT resources are usually inexpensive, they should be considered as a first option by library media specialists when addressing students' learning needs. A variety of low tech products can be made available in the library for trial purposes with minimal investment. Some ready-made low-tech kits can be purchased through commercial vendors. Onion Mountain Technology, Inc., <http://www.onionmountaintech.com> produces a series of low- and mid-tech educational AT kits. These kits can be purchased through the company's Web site. Low-tech solutions for learning include some of the following techniques and products:

- Math
  - Manipulative objects for grouping and counting
  - Graph paper for numeric alignment
  - Math fact and measurement charts and matrices
  - Color-coding techniques for reference handouts
  - Sample problem displays or cards
  - Math concepts printed on removable labels for ease of access

- Reading
  - Reading frames and bookmarks
  - Guided reading techniques and outline sheets
  - Colored overlays
  - Erasable highlighters
  - Highlighting tape
  - Large print materials
  - Magnification sheets and lenses

- Writing
  - Erasable pens
  - Pen and pencil grips
  - Scribing services
  - Wide ruled paper
  - Carbon paper for note taking assistance
  - No carbon required (NCR) paper for note taking assistance
  - Paper stabilizers

- Organization
  - Graphic organizers
  - Color coding
  - Removable sticky notes
  - Personal planning booklets and calendars
  - Assignment and planning rubrics
  - Binders with subject dividers and supply pouches
  - Adhesive Velcro to secure loose objects
  - Timers and cuing systems

- Keyboarding
  - Large print, and color-coded or invisible Braille key labels
  - Key guards
  - Keyboard skins
  - Monitor screen visors and peripheral magnifiers
  - Document and book holders with magnification or highlighting devices

High Tech

According to the *TechEncyclopedia of TechWeb* <http://content.techweb.com/encyclopedia/defineterm?term=hightech nology>, high technology "Refers to the latest advancements in computers and electronics as well as to the social and political environment and consequences created by such machines." This is an exciting time in education. Advances in technology are leveling the playing field for more and more of our students with disabilities. It is important for educators to be aware of new assistive technologies and develop networks for sharing information about what is working.

Desktop and laptop computers have become increasingly powerful devices. These computers can be equipped with assistive technologies to provide improved access to learning for struggling students. Examples of high-tech AT hardware and software will be covered in Chapters 8 through 14.

School Reform Initiatives and U.S. Legislation

At the same time that schools are expected to accommodate a growing percentage of special needs students, there are increasing demands for improved student performance on standardized tests. School success is frequently measured according to comparative academic outcomes. However, the pressure to raise the overall academic standing of students in a school may be a challenge to reconcile with inclusive school practices.

Schools that are highly successful in providing special needs students with the opportunities and support they need to participate in regular academic programs may rank lower in comparative analyses of student academic performance. Taxpayers, education critics, administrators, teachers, and the school community need to view the academic performance of schools in relation to the obligations of schools to provide all students with the opportunity to reach their learning potential.

The concept of universal design for learning (UDL) is based on the premise that curriculum activities, assignments, and materials should be flexible and versatile in order to accommodate a variety of learners and learning styles. As educators are aware that students have different learning strengths and preferences, they have worked to provide visual, auditory, and hands-on learning experiences for students. Schools that strive to apply UDL concepts to all areas of student learning take into account access issues for students with disabilities and for students with various learning styles. The task for educators in successfully implementing UDL is to identify and remove barriers to learning within the learning environment. The goal of UDL is educational access for all students. The Center for Applied Special Technology (CAST) has a collection of valuable resources, articles, and "best practice" examples of universal design for learning on its Web site <http://www.cast.org>. The book *Teaching Every Student in the Digital Age: Universal Design for Learning* (Rose, D., Meyer, A., 2002) is available online <http://www.cast.org/teachingeverystudent/ ideas/tes/>. This very accessible resource provides extensive information on the rationale and implementation of universal design for learning.

No Child Left Behind (NCLB)

The development of accountability measures for K–12 education is a growing trend in many education systems around the world today. In the United States, a nationwide initiative to promote accountability and improve student performance has been launched by the Bush administration. The No Child Left Behind (NCLB) Act of 2001, signed into law by President Bush on January 8, 2002 (Public Law 107-110), is the reauthorization of the Elementary and Secondary Education Act (ESEA). Although NCLB is still based on ESEA, there are a number of significant changes that will challenge states and districts during the early implementation period, which started during the 2002–2003 school year. The ultimate goal of NCLB is for 100% of students to be proficient on annual state assessments in reading, math, and science by the end of the 2013–2014 school year.

Students are not the only ones expected to meet standards under NCLB. All teachers must be "highly qualified" by the end of the 2005–2006 school year. Emphasis will also be placed on assessment and accountability measures for schools receiving Title I funds to improve the academic achievement of disadvantaged students. See *No Child Left Behind: A Desktop Reference* <http://www.ed.gov/offices/ OESE/reference.html> for information on Title I and other aspects of the No Child Left Behind Act of 2001.

District and school accountability requirements demand that states must define what will constitute *adequate yearly progress* for measuring school performance. Once that measurement starting point is determined, the baseline must be incrementally raised over the 12-year period so that 100% of students reach proficiency by 2014. A summary of the major elements of NCLB has been produced by the Washington, D.C.-based *Learning First Alliance* <http://learningfirst.org/pdfs/ nochildleft.pdf>.

Individuals with Disabilities Education Act (IDEA)

The Individuals with Disabilities Education Act (IDEA) contains specific information that educators must be aware of with respect to assistive technology entitlement for students with disabilities:

> *Section § 300.5 Assistive technology device*
> *As used in this part, **Assistive technology device** means any item, piece of equipment, or product system, whether acquired commercially off the shelf, modified, or customized, that is used to increase, maintain, or improve the functional capabilities of a child with a disability (Authority: 20 U.S.C. 1401(1)).*

> *Section § 300.6 Assistive technology service*
> *As used in this part, **Assistive technology service** means any service that directly assists a child with a disability in the selection, acquisition, or use of an assistive technology device.*
> *The term include—*
> > *(a) The evaluation of the needs of a child with a disability, including a functional evaluation of the child in the child's customary environment;*
> > *(b) Purchasing, leasing, or otherwise providing for the acquisition of assistive technology devices by children with disabilities;*
> > *(c) Selecting, designing, fitting, customizing, adapting,*

applying, maintaining, repairing, or replacing assistive technology devices;

(d) Coordinating and using other therapies, interventions, or services with assistive technology devices, such as those associated with existing education and rehabilitation plans and programs;

(e) Training or technical assistance for a child with a disability or, if appropriate, that child's family; and

(f) Training or technical assistance for professionals (including individuals providing education or rehabilitation services), employers, or other individuals who provide services to, employ, or are otherwise substantially involved in the major life functions of that child (Authority: 20 U.S.C. 1401(2)); IDEA '97 Final Regulations.

IDEA also specifies that students who have an Individual Education Plan (IEP) must be considered for assistive technology.

Section § 300.346 Development, review and revision of IEP

(a) Development of IEP.

  (1) General. In developing each child's IEP, the IEP team, shall consider—

   (i) The strengths of the child and the concerns of the parents for enhancing the education of their child;

   (ii) The results of the initial or most recent evaluation of the child; and

   (iii)As appropriate, the results of the child's performance on any general State or district-wide assessment programs.

  (2) Consideration of special factors. The IEP team also shall—

   (i) In the case of a child whose behavior impedes his or her learning or that of others, consider, if appropriate, strategies, including positive behavioral interventions, strategies, and supports to address that behavior;

   (ii) In the case of a child with limited English proficiency, consider the language needs of the child as those needs relate to the child's IEP;

   (iii)In the case of a child who is blind or visually impaired, provide for instruction in Braille and the use of Braille unless the IEP

team determines, after an evaluation of the child's reading and writing skills, needs, and appropriate reading and writing media (including an evaluation of the child's future needs for instruction in Braille or the use of Braille), that instruction in Braille or the use of Braille is not appropriate for the child;

(iv) Consider the communication needs of the child, and in the case of a child who is deaf or hard of hearing, consider the child's language and communication needs, opportunities for direct communications with peers and professional personnel in the child's language and communication mode, academic level, and full range of needs, including opportunities for direct instruction in the child's language and communication mode; and

(v) Consider whether the child requires assistive technology devices and services.

(b) Review and Revision of IEP. In conducting a meeting to review, and, if appropriate, revise a child's IEP, the IEP team shall consider the factors described in paragraph (a) of this section.

(c) Statement in IEP. If, in considering the special factors described in paragraphs (a)(1) and (2) of this section, the IEP team determines that a child needs a particular device or service (including an intervention, accommodation, or other program modification) in order for the child to receive FAPE, the IEP team must include a statement to that effect in the child's IEP.

(d) Requirement with respect to regular education teacher. The regular education teacher of a child with a disability, as a member of the IEP team, must, to the extent appropriate, participate in the development, review, and revision of the child's IEP, including assisting in the determination of—

(1) Appropriate positive behavioral interventions and strategies for the child; and

(2) Supplementary aids and services, program modifications or supports for school personnel that will be provided for the child, consistent with 300.347(a)(3).

(e) Construction. Nothing in this section shall be construed to require the IEP team to include

information under one component of a child's IEP that is already contained under another component of the child's IEP (Authority: 20 U.S.C. 1414(d)(3) and (4)(B) and (e)); IDEA '97 Final Regulations.

Under IDEA there is an obligation to provide assistive technology if the IEP team has determined that AT is necessary to provide a free appropriate public education (FAPE) in the least restrictive environment (LRE). The decision as to what form of education is "appropriate" and "least restrictive" will vary from student to student. There is certainly the potential for differences in opinion over these terms. However, the school library media center, as an integral part of the school's learning environment, should be equipped to support the learning needs of as many special needs students as possible. Making accessible technology available in the school library media center is essential to reducing the barriers to learning for special needs students.

Section § 300.308 Assistive technology
(a) Each public agency shall ensure that assistive technology devices or assistive technology services, or both, as those terms are defined in §§300.5-300.6, are made available to a child with a disability if required as a part of the child's—
(1) Special education under §300.26;
(2) Related services under §300.24; or
(3) Supplementary aids and services under §§300.28 and 300.550(b)(2).
(b) On a case-by-case basis, the use of school-purchased assistive technology devices in a child's home or in other settings is required if the child's IEP team determines that the child needs access to those devices in order to receive FAPE (Authority: 20 U.S.C. 1412(a)(12)(B)(i)).

Least Restrictive Environment (LRE)
Section § 300.550 General LRE requirements
(a) Except as provided in §300.311(b) and (c), a State shall demonstrate to the satisfaction of the Secretary that the State has in effect policies and procedures to ensure that it meets the requirements of §§300.550-300.556.
(b) Each public agency shall ensure—
(1) That to the maximum extent appropriate, children with disabilities, including children in public or private institutions or other care

facilities, are educated with children who are nondisabled; and

(2) That special classes, separate schooling or other removal of children with disabilities from the regular educational environment occurs only if the nature or severity of the disability is such that education in regular classes with the use of supplementary aids and services cannot be achieved satisfactorily (Authority: 20 U.S.C. 1412(a)(5)); IDEA '97 Final Regulations.

Rehabilitation Act of 1973 (Section 504), The Americans with Disabilities Act (ADA)

Both the Rehabilitation Act (Section 504) and the Americans with Disabilities Act prohibit public entities, such as schools, and other recipients of federal funds from discriminating against persons with disabilities. These laws require schools to make their buildings and programs, both academic and non-academic, equally accessible to students with disabilities (Chapter IV—Education-Related Sources of Assistive Technology Funding, ***Paying For The Assistive Technology You Need: A Consumer Guide to Funding Sources in Washington State***, Developed and produced by the University of Washington for the Washington Assistive Technology Alliance (WATA), 2002). Together with the IDEA, the Rehabilitation Act (Section 504) and the ADA are in place to ensure that students receive a free appropriate public education (FAPE) in the least restrictive environment (LRE).

The Council for Exceptional Children has published the ***Discover IDEA CD 2002***. This resource includes information about the Individuals with Disabilities Education Act, No Child Left Behind, and other helpful resources. It has been designed for ease of navigation with keyword search capabilities. More information about this resource can be found at <http://www.ideapractices.org/resources/detail.php?id=2038>.

References

Baumel, Jan, ***Answers to Questions about Special Education Protections: FAPE, LRE, IEE, Due Process***, September 13, 2002 <http://www.schwablearning.org/articles.asp?g=2&r=625>.

IDEA '97 Final Regulations, 34 CFR Part 300, Assistance to States for the Education of Children With Disabilities, (Part B of the Individuals with Disabilities Education Act), Subpart A-General <http://www.ideapractices.org/law/regulations/topicIndex.php>.

Major Changes to ESEA in the No Child Left Behind Act, Learning First Alliance, Washington, D.C., January 2002 <http://learningfirst.org/pdfs/nochildleft.pdf>.

No Child Left Behind: A Desktop Reference, U.S. Department of Education <http://www.ed.gov/offices/OESE/reference.html>.

No Child Left Behind Act of 2001: Reauthorization of the Elementary and Secondary Education Act, Council for Exceptional Children, Oct. 2, 2002 <http://www.cec.sped.org/pp/OverviewNCLB.pdf>.

Paying For The Assistive Technology You Need: A Consumer Guide to Funding Sources in Washington State, Developed and produced by the University of Washington for the Washington Assistive Technology Alliance (WATA), 2002 <http://uwctds.washington.edu/funding%20manual/index.htm#begin>.

Rose, David H. & Meyer, Anne, ***Teaching Every Student in the Digital Age: Universal Design for Learning***, ASCD 2002 <http://www.cast.org/teachingeverystudent/ideas/tes/>.

TechEncyclopedia of TechWeb, <http://content.techweb.com/encyclopedia/ defineterm?term= hightechnology>.

Technology-Related Assistance For Individuals With Disabilities Act Of 1988 As Amended In 1994, Section 3. Definitions (Public Laws 100-407 and 103-218) <http://www.resna.org/taproject/library/laws/techact94.htm>.

Chapter 3

The Role of Assistive Technology in Schools

Schools have a duty to provide all students with access to the curriculum and to prepare them to lead productive lives. Appropriate assistive technology leads to greater independence and provides access to lifelong learning for people with disabilities.

The numbers of students with disabilities in the education system has grown. In the 1999–2000 school year, almost 6.5 million children in the United States between zero and 21 years of age received services under the Individuals with Disabilities Education Act, compared to just 3.7 million in 1977 (*Twenty-five Years of Educating Children with Disabilities: The Good News and the Work Ahead 2002*, 2001). Successful inclusion of these students is a priority. Educators are still learning to adjust.

There are challenges ahead for educators in creating a system that addresses the needs of students with disabilities. *Twenty-five Years of Educating Children with Disabilities: The Good News and the Work Ahead 2002*, a publication of the American Youth Policy Forum and Center on Education Policy, identifies 10 challenges facing education policy-makers and educators in educating students with disabilities:

- Challenge 1—Participation in the General Curriculum
- Challenge 2—Higher Achievement
- Challenge 3—Over-Representation of Minority Students
- Challenge 4—High School Graduation
- Challenge 5—Postsecondary Enrollment and Completion

- ■ Challenge 6—Preparation for Employment
- ■ Challenge 7—Teacher Development
- ■ Challenge 8—Paperwork and Procedural Requirements
- ■ Challenge 9—Access to Technology
- ■ Challenge 10—Other Work Ahead

Challenge 9 identifies the importance of providing access to technology for special needs students. The report emphasizes that many children who could benefit from AT and Internet-based technologies do not have access to them. It also states that technology is an area where special education teachers report feeling least skillful. New initiatives and resources need to be introduced to change this situation. Data from 1998 indicates that 52% of U.S. public school teachers did not participate in any professional development related to special needs students during the prior 12 months (*Twenty-five Years of Educating Children with Disabilities: The Good News and the Work Ahead 2002*, 2001).

The Functional Role of Assistive Technology

Assistive technology use leads to new opportunities. Students not only develop knowledge and skills related to the computer technology itself, they also gain access to efficient methods for connecting with others, researching, sending, and receiving information.

Access to Information

Information helps us to make appropriate decisions. A person who has a disability may have a disadvantage in gaining access to information. People who live with a disability must find ways to compensate for their areas of challenge by strengthening themselves in other ways, or taking advantage of enabling resources. Adversity is a catalyst for exploring innovative ways to accomplish a task or solve a problem.

Students with disabilities, as well as nondisabled students, need to be encouraged to look for alternatives. Improved access to information resources through alternative formats, Internet access, and assistive technologies provide students with more options for creating their own pathways to achievement. Computer and other assistive technologies are tools that help students with disabilities take control of their lives. Personal growth and creativity are enhanced through independent access to information.

Access to the Curriculum

Students who are given few alternatives for learning find themselves in a bind if alternative AT resources are inaccessible to them. For example, when the primary means of delivering information is a textbook, students with reading and visual disabilities are at a disadvantage. These students will not experience optimal learning unless there are other supports or learning alternatives available to them.

The following articles emphasize the value of flexible curriculum materials, especially the benefits of digital text. Digital text resources can be manipulated more easily than print resources to meet the needs of students with disabilities.

- *A Curriculum Every Student Can Use: Design Principles For Student Access* <http://www.cec.sped.org/osep/ud-sec1.html> offers a series of informative online articles dealing with curriculum access issues. These articles emphasize that accessible curriculum design provides improved learning opportunities for a wide range of students, not just students with disabilities.
- The National Center on Accessing the General Curriculum has prepared a series of articles: *Technical Brief: Access, Participation, and Progress in the General Curriculum* <http://www.cast.org/ncac/Access,Participation,andProgressintheGeneralCurriculum2830.cfm>.

The Value of AT for Educators

In an ideal world, all curriculum materials would be designed with built-in accessibility features. While some companies are making an effort to develop learning materials that do have accessibility options, we have not yet reached that point for the majority of classroom and library learning materials. Instead of flexible materials that have ready-made options for students with various learning preferences, we usually rely on reference materials and textbooks that present learning barriers for some students.

It is time consuming and inconvenient for a teacher or library media specialist to have to convert print materials to an accessible format. The time it takes to photocopy and enlarge the print in a textbook chapter is onerous when compared with the rapid conversion to large print when a digital textbook is available. A student with a low vision condition can enlarge digital text in a few seconds on the computer screen. The student with a reading disability can have the computer read the digital text to him or her with the application of a screen reading utility. These have time saving benefits for the instructor and are skills that the students can repeatedly employ for lifelong information access.

Accessible learning materials assist educators in the following ways:

- They save time compared to modifying standard print materials for individual students. This reduces teacher workload and the pressure to invent individualized materials.
- The ability to modify the curriculum material is available to the student, which again reduces the need for teacher intervention.
- They help to vary the presentation options available to all students, which reduces the stigma individual students may feel when presented with modified materials.
- They promote overall classroom awareness about diverse learning needs and accessibility options.

One example of an accessible learning resource is *The Digital Field Trip to The Rainforest AT*, an accessible multimedia digital field trip on CD. Developed by Digital Frog International Inc., of Puslinch, Ontario, Canada, the CD has been designed for use with three different modes of operation: Standard, Text-To-Speech, and Text-To-Speech without a mouse. The product is also compatible with some add-on screen magnification products so that students with visual impairments can access the information. This resource allows students with visual disabilities or certain mobility, learning, or language challenges to work side by side with nondisabled students. It does not require the teacher to adjust the learning materials. The options to modify the content are built into the software. This gives each student control over how he or she wants to receive the information. There are also digital worksheets available on the CD. These are available in PDF and *MS Word* formats. These options allow educators to quickly select and modify exercises. More information about this product is available through Digital Frog International Inc. <http://www.digitalfrog.com>.

Social and Psychological Value of AT for Students

A welcoming tone is set when learning materials are created with the needs of all students in mind. Students with special needs frequently rely on advocates, teacher aides, or parents to negotiate for the supports that they need. It is a relief to these students to find resources that they can independently access.

Skill Development and Specialization
Everyone needs to feel capable of setting and achieving personal goals. Achievable goals must be determined on an individual basis. Learning new AT skills encourages relevant goal setting for a student with a

disability. Learning ways to function more productively through well matched AT, and observing others who have acquired AT skills, can provide strong motivation. When students extend their abilities through technology, there is bound to be a realization that new goals can be accomplished. Task accomplishment provides a healthy measure of encouragement for students who have struggled with learning tasks. Positive AT results lead to new possibilities and provide a means for the user to establish new goals.

Students who develop advanced knowledge and skills in a specialized area of assistive technology will be valued resource people who are capable of helping others to apply that knowledge for new purposes. Knowing that others can benefit from one's expertise reinforces a student's sense of self-worth and value to the community. The ability to instruct others through specialist skills and knowledge brings with it the power to influence. The ability to influence attracts people who can help to accomplish collaborative goals.

Competency and Independence

A student who has mastered basic AT skills can pursue higher levels of skill acquisition. Wheelchair athletes are a great example of how mastery of a mobility device can lead to highly skilled participation and competitive opportunities. Assistive technology helps students strive for independence and enhanced performance. Assistive technology alleviates the frustration of having to be completely reliant on another person to assist with tasks that students would rather perform themselves. Progress toward greater independence provides a sense of relief for these students and their caregivers.

Self-Esteem and Peace of Mind

Finding ways to build self-esteem, the equivalent of elevating a student's feeling of worth, is part of an educator's job. Assistive technology allows a student to contribute through participation or communication. Putting forward an effort and being recognized for one's contribution reinforces a person's sense of self-value. Assistive technology can create pathways toward a positive self-image.

Well-matched assistive technology products can be valuable problem solvers for students with disabilities. Day-to-day challenges will still be present for a student with a disability, even with well selected AT. However, assistive technology creates new options for students, their families, and educators to help them overcome learning and daily living challenges.

Lifelong Tools Promote Participation

Assistive technology products continue to be developed and upgraded to meet the needs of consumers. With so many existing and emerging products available to suit a broad range of needs, AT evaluation must be considered as an ongoing process. Students' educational and developmental needs change over time. Therefore, AT adjustments may be necessary as a student grows and matures. Ongoing assistive technology development and design is leading to increasingly flexible product options and features. Consumers can feel optimistic that many new AT options will become available in the years ahead.

▶ Professional Perspective

Scott Bellman, MA, LMHC, CRC is Project Coordinator/Counselor for DO-IT (Disabilities, Opportunities, Internetworking, and Technology) at the University of Washington in Seattle, WA. Bellman is currently working at DO-IT on several projects that promote the inclusion of people with disabilities in science, technology, engineering, mathematics, and business. His interests include transition for high-school students, adaptive technology, self-empowerment for postsecondary students, and increasing accessibility on postsecondary campuses and employment settings. Bellman and some of his students responded to the following question:

Are high-school students with disabilities who transition with adaptive technology skills better prepared for the demands of postsecondary education and work?

High-school students vary in their ability to understand and utilize adaptive technology for school and work. On one end of this spectrum are students who have had no exposure to adaptive hardware and software, contrasted with students at the other end who may have equipment at home, or devices that travel with them to classes or employment settings.

Upon graduation, high-school students with disabilities who are skilled at using technology, including adaptive technology if needed, are better prepared to engage in postsecondary study and employment. Technology skills are crucial for transitioning students as they increase their level of independence, consider programs of study and careers, and cope with a high volume of new material as a freshman in college or as a new employee at a work site. Knowledge about adaptive technology may also be seen by certain employers as an important and hard-to-find skill set, and, therefore, increase the job applicant's chances of being noticed.

Increasing Independence

As high-school graduates engage in work and postsecondary programs of study, they may find themselves in the new role of self-advocate. For most students, this situation is in sharp contrast to high school, where parents and teachers played the primary roles as advocates.

Strong technology skills, including adaptive technology for many, are essential as students come to embrace their new independence. Such skills allow students to find resources over the Internet, engage in correspondence, and organize their thoughts and activities. As reported by one community college student with cerebral palsy and learning disability:

> "I wish that I could have understood better that you do most of your work outside of the class. I would have had a hard time if I had not known about adaptive technology before college. I use it about every day now to write papers and I also use it to talk to my professors."

Both new college students and new employees take on tasks that weren't required in high school. For instance, they may be asked to generate reports, manipulate data, or engage in advanced research. A thorough understanding of mainstream hardware, software, and adaptive technology options will help these students tackle new types of assignments. As reported by a computer science college student who is blind:

> "Knowledge about adaptive technology is crucial in transitioning from high school to higher education and work. Knowledge of these devices assisted me in attending college, as I was more able to independently complete my assignments and other tasks by scanning handouts, using online course Web sites, and typing, editing, and printing assignments. My Braille Lite, a note taking device, allows me to take and review lecture notes, as well as access documents needed for in-class activities."

Selecting Programs of Study and Careers

When persons with disabilities think about postsecondary study and employment, they will need to imagine themselves in new environments. Part of this process involves researching schools and organizations to understand what support services are available. Adaptive technology can play an important part in this research. As stated by a computer science college student who is blind:

> "The more skills a high-school student can have before leaving, the better prepared he [or she] will be for college or for anything else. Also, the knowledge is important when deciding on a college, and deciding what needs to be obtained either from the college or other resources."

Work-based learning opportunities, which require the use of technology, help high-school students with disabilities learn to apply technology in different situations. This knowledge will prepare them for future school and work environments, where they will use adaptive technology and request reasonable accommodations.

New Learning Challenges

College freshman are typically overwhelmed with new challenges. They need to engage in good problem solving for dealing with housing, course selection, new relationships, food and nutrition, finances, and transportation—just to name a few. Students who are immersed in this difficult environment should be ready to apply their adaptive technology skills. The same can be said for students accepting a new job. As summarized by a computer science college student who is blind:

> *"It is important that the student know what works for him [or her] in the classroom and also outside of the classroom. College is not a time to be learning these things over again. Or rather, not to be learning what one could have had in high school."*

Adaptive Technology Skills Attract Certain Employers

Some employers are aware of the need to better serve their customers with disabilities. Graduating high-school students with disabilities can promote their knowledge of adaptive technology to employers as a unique and valuable skill. As stated by a technical support specialist and college graduate who is blind:

> *"When I worked at the library, I trained the staff [members] on the different kinds of adaptive technology that disabled people use and showed them how to use the library tools in conjunction with speech and the keyboard. This made it possible for them to teach visually impaired users who came to the library. Today, I am updating and troubleshooting Access databases. I will eventually be training a volunteer who is visually impaired."*

References

A Curriculum Every Student Can Use: Design Principles For Student Access, ERIC/OSEP Topical Brief—Fall 1998 <http://www.cec.sped.org/osep/ud-sec1.html>.

Americans with Disabilities, U.S. Department of Commerce, Economics and Statistics Administration, U.S. Census Bureau <http://www.census.gov/prod/2001pubs/p70-73.pdf>.

Technical Brief: Access, Participation, and Progress in the General Curriculum, The National Center on Accessing the General Curriculum <http://www.cast.org/ncac/Access,Participation, andProgressintheGeneralCurriculum2830.cfm>.

Twenty-five Years of Educating Children with Disabilities: The Good News and the Work Ahead 2002, Washington, D.C.: American Youth Policy Forum and Center on Education Policy, 2001 <http://www.aypf.org/publications/special_ed/Special_Ed.pdf>.

Chapter 4

Assistive Technology Teams

In an ideal world, there would be unlimited resources to support the diverse technology needs of all students. In the real world, decisions have to be made based on budgetary realities. There are competing demands for technology funds from many departments within the modern school. In jurisdictions outside the United States, where AT service delivery is not a legal obligation, educators who work with special needs students must make their technology needs known to administrators so that AT is not overlooked. Administrators who have influence over funding decisions are essential members of the assistive technology team.

Part of the reason for adopting a team approach to AT decision making is to ensure that technology funds are well spent. However, the needs of the students are the most important reasons for establishing teams to consider appropriate assistive technology trials, training, and acquisitions. Assistive technology assessment is an ongoing process for groups of students, as well as for individual students.

Although the team AT assessment and selection process is considered the best approach to delivering assistive technology services, it may not be possible or practical in all circumstances.

▶ AT Team and Guidelines

Ideally, an AT team will be comprised of educator, parent, and student participants, where appropriate. However, the lone decision maker may be the only option in some circumstances. When there is a tight time line for making technology purchases with insufficient time for team consultation, one person will have to make the spending decisions. In these situations, advice from colleagues, students, or parents may be sought quickly through a variety of methods including e-mail surveys, informal focus groups, or staff questionnaires. This informal team input can help to facilitate or reinforce an individual decision about AT purchases in these circumstances.

Increasingly, schools and districts are moving to a formal team approach for student AT assessment and decision making. As an example, the New York State AT Guidelines are available through the Technology Resources for Education (TRE) Center Web site <http://www.trecenter.org/guidelines.htm#desc>. One of its online resources is called *Assistive Technology Assessment: A Team Approach* <http://www.trecenter.org/appendixA.htm>.

The team should consider a range of possible AT solutions, not focus on one technology or strategy to "fix" the problem. This necessitates the inclusion of one or more people who are knowledge-able about assistive technology. It may be necessary to bring in a district specialist or consultant if there is no one on staff with adequate AT knowledge to lead the assessment. Some districts facilitate the process through the use of videoconferencing technologies, which connect experts to school-based teams.

The concept of an "extended consultation" requires that the student have the opportunity to be involved in a lengthy trial of the product, if necessary, to facilitate appropriate decisions. Finally, consultative follow-up is an important part of the process that is frequently neglected by AT teams. Often a decision is made to implement assistive technology for a student without a plan for evaluating this decision at regular intervals. If there is no follow-up to the process, the student may become frustrated and abandon the device or software. Without follow-up, the AT team is unaware that the AT "solution" has been abandoned by the student. When this occurs, the team continues to function, oblivious to the consequences of its decisions and without an opportunity to take corrective action that could resolve the problems.

In jurisdictions outside the United States, where AT services are not legally required, professionals may find themselves implementing AT resources and services in an informal structure through their own initiatives. These AT pioneers may have to find their "teams" and support systems outside of their work environment. A number of Internet discussion groups devoted to collegial support and AT knowledge sharing have been established. These forums provide opportunities for educators, who feel professionally or geographically isolated, to connect with others who share their interests in assistive technology.

Where possible, the selection of AT team members should also reflect the source of the funding. Representatives of a funding source should have an opportunity to react to the proposed allocation of their funds. This consideration has the benefit of ensuring that the agency or benefactor is supportive of the purchase process and will be inclined to approve a future request for funds.

AT Mini-Assessment

The Alliance for Technology Access (ATA) is a national organization located in San Rafael, California. Its membership includes AT resource centers, individual and organizational associates, as well as AT developers and vendors. ATA has some good resources available online <http://www.ataccess.org/resources/atk12/default.html>. The *Assistive Technology in K–12 Schools* Web page has many helpful links to documents and other sites including the AT Mini-Assessment <http://www.ataccess.org/resources/atk12/miniassessment.html>. Schools completing this assessment give themselves a one to five ranking on seven essential qualities for high quality AT service. Highly satisfactory services receive a score of one. A score of five indicates that the quality being assessed needs improvement. Schools with low scores are considered to be providing satisfactory to superior AT services. Resource links are provided on the assessment page to give direction to schools not performing well on the assessment. This assessment tool could help staff to focus on areas for improvement and provide direction for policies, professional development, and funding issues. Some departments may have implemented AT or strategies that could be shared with their colleagues in other areas of the school. This assessment form could also be used as a model for developing a more specialized internal AT assessment tool for a K–12 library media center.

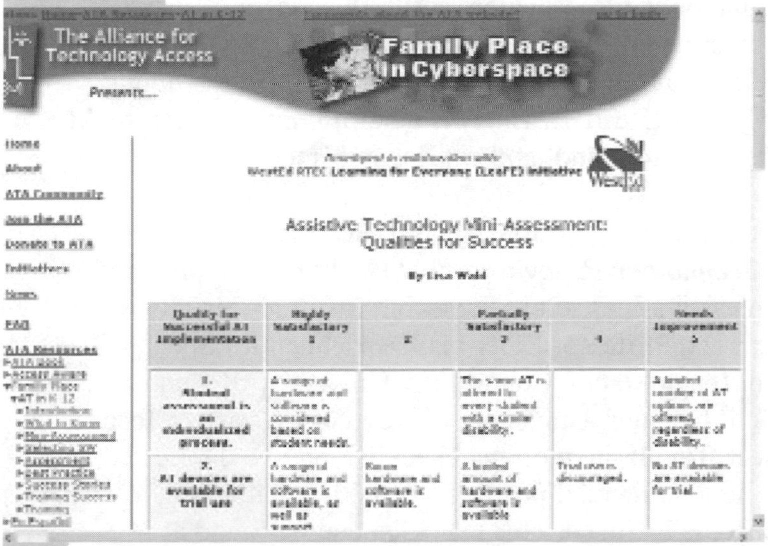

Figure 4.1: Assistive Technology Mini-Assessment
[Used with permission. Developed by Lisa Wahl for the Alliance for Technology Access. Funded by WestEd <http://www.ataccess.org/resources/atk12/default.html>.]

Quality Indicators for Assistive Technology

The Quality Indicators for Assistive Technology Services is a document collaboratively developed by the Quality Indicators for Assistive

Technology (QIAT) Consortium. The document has been updated since it was first developed in 1998. The current QIAT Quality Indicators 2002 is available at <http://sweb.uky.edu/~jszaba0/qiatqualityind00.html>.

This document provides quality indicator guidelines for:

- Administrative Support
- Consideration of Assistive Technology Needs
- Assessment of Assistive Technology Needs
- Documentation in the IEP
- Assistive Technology Implementation
- Evaluation of Effectiveness

Each of these sub-sections also provides a summary of the common errors that may accompany AT service development and delivery. This information helps to create awareness about unforeseen issues related to AT services.

Education Tech Points Framework

A 450-page manual, *Education Tech Points: A Framework for Assistive Technology Planning (Bowser, G., Reed, P.)*, is designed to help school districts provide appropriate assistive technology services for students with special needs. More detail on this manual can be found online <http://www.edtechpoints.org/manual.htm>.

An online student workbook, *Hey Can I Try That?*, is available on the Education Tech Points Web site <http://www.edtechpoints.org/>. The authors, Gayl Bowser and Penny Reed, grant permission to print and copy this resource as long as credit is maintained. Another resource guide is available online to educators at the Wisconsin Assistive Technology Initiative (WATI) site <http://www.wati.org/resourceguide.htm>. *A Resource Guide for Teachers and Administrators about Assistive Technology* (Reed, P., 2001) is a helpful introduction to AT that can be shared with school and district staff members.

Assistive Technology Policy Checklist

The *Assistive Technology Policy Checklist* (© 2001) was prepared for the National Assistive Technology Research Institute (NATRI) by A. Edward Blackhurst, Professor Emeritus, Department of Special Education and Rehabilitation Counseling, University of Kentucky, and Jennifer K. Bell, Director, University of Kentucky Assistive Technology (UKAT) Project. The 85-item online checklist may be duplicated and circulated for noncommercial purposes, provided that credit, as stated on the Web page, is included. This checklist can be found at <http://natri.uky.edu/resources/reports/cheklst.html>.

The Assistive Technology Checklist is a tool to be used for developing, analyzing, or obtaining feedback regarding the appropriateness of AT policies. The 85-item checklist is organized under 13 element categories: Conceptual, Assistive Technology, Legal, Empirical, Theoretical, Normative, Economic, Political, Cultural, Ideological, Historical, Logical, and Assumptive.

Assessment Methods

Assistive technology assessments can be accomplished through formal and informal methods. There are differences between doing an AT assessment for an individual and reviewing the accessibility of a classroom or library media center. The AT needs of a special needs student must be considered in his or her Individual Education Plan (IEP). IEP recommendations may lead to specific recommendations regarding the student's ability to access library media center resources. Some students may bring their own AT with them to the library media center for individual use. However, this is not always a practical solution.

Selecting appropriate assistive technology for general use within the library media center will focus on identifying and eliminating barriers to information, learning, and library resources. Library AT should be selected in consultation with the special education staff, as this helps to identify the AT needs of the student population. It will also prevent expenditures on products that students already have access to and are able to bring with them to the library media center.

Collaborative library AT planning will be more efficient if it involves a staff member or consultant who is knowledgeable about appropriate AT options. Some structured assessment methods have been developed to guide the process. These tools have been designed for individual AT assessments, but knowledge of these resources may be helpful in focusing discussion about library media center accessibility and AT.

SETT (Student, Environment, Task, Tool) Framework

The SETT Framework <http://sweb.uky.edu/~jszaba0/JoySETT.html>, developed by Joy Zabala, provides an easy to follow outline to help support the AT assessment and intervention process. SETT stands for four essential AT consideration components: Student, Environment, Task, and Tools. The SETT acronym simplifies the process of assessment by reminding AT teams to take a broad view of students' educational needs. AT teams must consider the characteristics of students, the natural settings where students will be learning and functioning, and the performance goals and tasks to be accomplished. Once these factors have been identified, the AT team can focus on appropriate AT options.

FEAT (Functional Evaluation for Assistive Technology)

The Functional Evaluation for Assistive Technology (FEAT) has recently been developed as the first standardized method for AT assessment specifically for individuals with learning disabilities. Co-developed by Marshall H. Raskind and Brian R. Bryant, the FEAT's five assessment forms may be completed by an individual or an AT team. The FEAT forms, in their typical order of completion, include:

- Contextual Matching Inventory
- Checklist of Strengths and Limitations
- Checklist of Technology Experiences
- Technology Characteristics Inventory
- Individual-Technology Evaluation Scale

Although the FEAT provides numeric rating scales, it is not designed as a test. The FEAT would best be described as a standardized evaluation of a person's AT needs. The FEAT was developed with input from professionals across the United States for the purpose of helping AT evaluators assist individuals to achieve greater independence. It is a well-organized system, adaptable for widespread use as a standardized assessment model. Most importantly, the FEAT's structure takes into consideration the multiple factors that demand flexibility in order to achieve successful AT outcomes. More information is available through the FEAT publisher, Psycho-Educational Services <http://www.psycho-educational.com>.

Assistive Technology Consideration Quick Wheel

The AT Quick Wheel is a resource authored by the IDEA Local Implementation by Local Administrators (ILIAD) Partnership, the Technology and Media (TAM) Division of the Council for Exceptional Children (CEC), and the Wisconsin Assistive Technology Initiative. Further information about the AT Wheel can be found online <http://www.ideapractices.org/resources/detail.php?id=22166>. The wheel provides a compact reference on U.S. federal definitions of AT devices and services as well as generic listings of assistive technology options for writing, computer access, math, and reading. The AT Quick Wheel was published in late 2002 and can be ordered from the Council for Exceptional Children (CEC) for $7.95 each for orders of 1–49, or $2.50 each for orders of 50 or more. Contact the CEC <service@cec.sped.org> for more information about placing an order for the AT Quick Wheel.

The challenge for professionals who work with special needs populations is to establish effective protocols for matching appropriate technologies to individual needs. Various forms, frameworks, and policies have been developed in different educational jurisdictions to ensure that the required assistive technology services are in place. As assistive technology is a relatively new area of specialization, it has been a challenge for professionals to find evaluation materials that promote a consistent approach to AT assessment. Recognize that assistive technology assessment and implementation must be an ongoing process. Student characteristics and the technology available to support students' special needs will continue to change over time.

References

Assistive Technology Assessment: A Team Approach, Assistive Technology Resources for New York State <http://www.trecenter.org/appendixA.htm>.

Bowser, G., Reed, P., *Education Tech Points: A Framework for Assistive Technology Planning* <http://www.edtechpoints.org/manual.htm>.

Quality Indicators for Assistive Technology Services, The QIAT Consortium <http://sweb.uky.edu/~jszaba0/qiatqualityind00.html>.

Zabala, J., *The SETT Framework: Critical Areas to Consider When Making Informed Assistive Technology Decisions* <http://sweb.uky.edu/~jszaba0/ SETTintro.html>.

Chapter 5

Assistive Technology Funding

Although the AT assessment process can be a daunting experience for educators unfamiliar with the field, it's often no less complex than the task of identifying and acquiring funding to implement AT. All members of the AT team may be in agreement that technology is necessary to enhance the accessibility of a school library media center for students with special needs. However, the price tag for the assistive technology may be prohibitive, unless the school is able to secure adequate funding, or free or low cost alternatives (see Chapter 9).

In addition to the maze of funding options that may or may not be available in your region, funding sources and opportunities are subject to change. For this reason, the information included in this section will be incomplete and will not apply to all educational jurisdictions. Educators will still have to do some detective work to find out which grants and funding they are eligible to receive.

Often, foundations target their funding or product support toward agencies that serve individuals with disabilities. For example, the Beaumont Foundation of America <http://www.bmtfoundation.com> grants Toshiba branded technology to help underserved populations in the United States. A total of $350 million in grants will be available in 2003 and 2004 as part of the foundation's commitment to the principle of digital inclusion, meaningful participation, and information literacy, with the mission of providing access to information for everyone, everywhere, anytime. Additional grants will be available in subsequent years. The foundation's three grant categories include community grants, education grants, and individual grants. Information about this grant program and its interesting history is available through the foundation's homepage and the grants page <http://www.bmtfoundation.com/grants/>.

The American Association of School Librarians has a link to awards, grants, and scholarships <http://www.ala.org/aasl/index.html>. Although these awards are not specifically linked to assistive technology initiatives, they can provide motivation for schools looking to implement innovative technology programs and partnerships.

Jurisdictional Funding Sources

The ABLEDATA Web site has an online resource to help reduce the work involved in tracking down available funding options. The *Informed Consumer's Guide to Funding Assistive Technology* <http://www.abledata.com/text2/funding.htm> lists contact information for each state technology assistance project in the United States. These organizations often collect information about funding sources that are available for their regions.

It is also helpful to understand the laws that relate to assistive technology funding in education. Chapter IV, *"Education-Related Sources Of Adaptive Technology Funding,"* from the online resource *Paying For The Assistive Technology You Need: A Consumer Guide to Funding Sources in Washington State* outlines the U.S. federal legislation that provides direction on student assistive technology entitlement and funding obligations of schools and school districts across the country. This manual is available online <http://uwctds.washington.edu/funding%20manual/index.htm#begin>.

Grant Seeking

A variety of established and newly created grant programs are helping educators obtain funding for assistive technology implementation. Up-to-date information on available grants can be found through Internet resources:

■ The *eSchool News Online* Funding Center is an excellent source of information about school technology grants and other funding sources. Informative articles about grant seeking are available on this site <http://www.eschoolnews.com/resources/funding/>.
■ *FundsNet Online Services* was created in 1996. It is a comprehensive listing of information on financial resources to help nonprofit organizations, colleges, and universities. Specific information on disability-focused funding as well as international

programs can be found through this excellent site
<http://www.fundsnetservices.com/>.

Government Sources

Educators in the United States have access to a considerable amount of federal education funding, which includes grants for assistive technology. Information about the U.S. Department of Education's Technology Grants Program is available online <http://www.ed.gov/Technology/edgrants.html>.

The U.S. Department of Education's **EDInfo** mailing list <http://www.ed.gov/MailingLists/EDInfo/> includes new postings on various funding opportunities. These updates can be read online or via a free e-mail subscription. The funding opportunities on this message list also include links to the application packages.

The U.S. Department of Education's Federal Register announcement page <http://www.ed.gov/legislation/FedRegister/announcements/index.html> provides updated information on grant competitions.

Similar federal education technology funding resources are not available in all countries. For example, there is no federal department of education in Canada, where K–12 education is strictly a provincial responsibility. Where provincial or other territorial governments administer education programs, the funding available for assistive technology varies greatly. In jurisdictions where assistive technology entitlement for K–12 students with disabilities is not defined in law, there may be very limited funding available through government sources. Therefore, a school's location, political, and socioeconomic circumstances will influence the decision to explore, and the success in securing funding support for assistive technology initiatives.

Corporate Sources

Many companies provide products or funding to support educational technology initiatives. Often, these programs are only available in the United States, although some corporations do provide technology and funding support to education systems outside the United States. **FundsNet Online Services** <http://www.fundsnetservices.com/>, mentioned earlier, is a good resource for researching corporate funding because the listings are updated regularly on this Web site.

A number of technology companies support schools and other nonprofit organizations with product donations through **Gifts in Kind International** <http://www.giftsinkind.org>. Click on "To Receive" to view the hardware and software vendors that donate their products through Gifts in Kind International. The Gifts in Kind homepage also has a link to an annual subscription-based grant seeking resource called *GrantStation*.

Funding and Grant Writing Resources

Major bookstores and online booksellers, such as Amazon.com, carry publications related to grant-seeking and funding agencies. Although books can provide a very good orientation to funding sources and the grant application process, it is unusual to find specific information on assistive technology funding in general grant-seeking manuals. Online resources are usually the best option for gathering current information and should be consulted as well. As funding information is subject to change, sole reliance on a book may prevent the grant seeker from pursuing unlisted or new funding opportunities.

Federal Money Retriever® <http://www.federalgrants.com> is a commercial software product designed to assist individuals and organizations interested in applying for U.S. government grants and loans. This product can be purchased in economy, standard, and professional versions. The higher-priced standard and professional versions include regular updates for a period of time, depending on the version purchased. As the U.S. Congress approves new federal funding twice yearly, the update versions allow users to learn of new funding opportunities. A keyword search of the software's database under "disabled, education" and "disabled, general" will bring up information on assistive technology funding. This product has received positive reviews for its ease of use, functionality, and low cost compared to hiring a consultant to research funding options.

A helpful resource for anyone new to grant seeking is the *Foundation Center* Web site <http://www.fdncenter.org/>. Go to the learning lab link to access the resources available through the virtual classroom. There are well-organized tutorials such as the "Proposal Writing Short Course," which provides a great introduction to the components of a standard proposal. Through the learning lab link, you'll also find the online librarian service. This allows you to send an online query regarding specific funding sources.

The *SchoolGrants* site <http://www.schoolgrants.org> offers a thorough and up-to-date collection of resources related to federal and state grants. There are links to government documents related to IDEA and No Child Left Behind legislation. You'll also find tips on how to prepare a successful grant proposal.

The "Funding Tips and Resources" page <http://www.techlearning.com/grants_res.html> of the *tech LEARNING* Web site <http://www.techlearning.com/> includes helpful links to funding agencies and searchable databases.

The Grantsmanship Center <http://www.tgci.com/> lists federal, state, community, and international grant information through the "grant sources" link.

DisabilityResources.org <http://www.disabilityresources.org/> is an excellent site with all kinds of information pertaining to a wide range of disability issues. At the top of the Web page is a link specifically for librarians. Make a point of visiting this page to find international links and numerous online resources. Look under "Popular Pages" on the right side of the homepage and you'll find information on grants and grant writing.

Case Study — Wisconsin Libraries Partner for Success
Learn How Schools and Community Libraries Can Work Together

Libraries in Wisconsin are making accessibility a priority. The Adams County Library in Adams, Wisconsin, was awarded a grant for 2002 entitled *Serving Children with Special Needs*. Adams County is one of 14 counties in Wisconsin where the child poverty rate is above 20%. Higher illiteracy rates are also found in this area. As this library is the only one in the county, its limited resources and Internet-connected computers with accessible features were in high demand.

The Adams County Library received $9,875 in federal funds under the Library Services and Technology Act (LSTA) through the Wisconsin Department of Public Instruction. Community partners were involved in the grant-application and resource-selection process. The Adams-Friendship Area Schools Early Childhood Program and Special Needs classrooms (preschool to high school) were important partners in this project.

The Adams County Library used the funding to purchase an adapted computer with specialized software. The library selected a *Dell* computer with a 16-inch monitor and touch screen, a color printer, a large key alphabetic keyboard, and a jellybean switch. This technology is located on a child-sized wheelchair-accessible computer table. The software available for use includes *ZoomText* magnification software as well as basic learning software. Other purchases included: books, magazines, and videos on children's special needs; adaptive toys and games; closed-caption videos; audiocassette kits; and child kits that include books with props such as puppets.

Another initiative launched by the Milwaukee Public Library (MPL) in partnership with the Milwaukee Public Schools (MPS) targets youth with learning disabilities. The MPL recognized a weakness in its services to these youth and contacted MPS about a possible partnership that would benefit from the school's expertise. The project improved library services through staff training, the purchase of new library materials including electronic resources, and a creative marketing plan directed at the target audience. Through the Wisconsin Department of Public Instruction, an LSTA grant of $21,130 was approved for the 2002 project *Learning for All: Service to Youth with Learning Disabilities*.

Collaboration with MPS Library Media Centers and the Special Services Division is viewed as an important part of the success of this project. School district specialists helped to train library staff about learning disabilities and assistive technology. Portable devices and *Start-to-Finish* reading kits were purchased along with software, which included *Write: Outloud* and *WYNN Reader*. Two promotional brochures were developed to educate the community about these new resources and were mailed to more than 800 school and community personnel. A Web site was created, and free kits containing more information and low-tech study aids were available to parents at MPL sites.

This project has contributed to its success in being chosen as a pilot site for the Hewlett-Packard (HP) Library Technology Access grant.

Learn More — Assistive Technology Grants

Ten Tips on Tech Funding

Sheryl Burgstahler, Ph.D., director of the University of Washington's DO-IT (Disabilities, Opportunities, Internetworking, and Technology) project, has authored grants and successfully secured funding from various foundations and agencies to support DO-IT. She also serves on grant review panels for the Office of Superintendent of Public Instruction, National Science Foundation, and U.S. Department of Education. Burgstahler lists 10 points that educators should keep in mind when exploring funding opportunities to support accessibility projects:

- Be sure you understand fully what types of projects the funding agency supports and what range of funding levels is usually provided.
- Conduct a literature review, summarize what projects/programs have been undertaken in your area of interest, and explain in your proposal why there is a need for your particular project.
- Develop a proposal that is beyond what is simply required by your school regarding the provision of accommodations for students with disabilities.
- Make sure that your goals and objectives are clear and that your proposed activities clearly support these goals and objectives.
- Avoid jargon and define terms that are not used by the general public.
- Format your proposal so that it is both easy to read straight through and easy to refer back to specific areas.
- Do not make promises you cannot deliver.
- Tell how the project activities (or at least some of them) will be sustained in your school after funding is complete.
- Tell how you will share project products and strategies with other organizations that have similar needs.
- Include a good evaluation plan that will determine if you reached the project objectives.

References

Hager, Ronald M., *Funding of Assistive Technology (The Public School's Special Education System as a Funding Source: The Cutting Edge)*, Neighborhood Legal Services, Inc., Buffalo, NY, 1999 <http://www.nls.org/specedat.htm>.

Paying For The Assistive Technology You Need: A Consumer Guide to Funding Sources in Washington State, Developed and produced by the University of Washington for the Washington Assistive Technology Alliance (WATA), 2002 <http://uwctds.washington.edu/funding%20manual/index.htm#begin>.

Wisconsin Department of Public Instruction (e-mail correspondence and primary document examination), March 2003.

Chapter 6

Accessibility Initiatives

Widespread use of computers and the Internet is leading to expanded accessibility initiatives such as online electronic text collections and related services for individuals with print disabilities. For people of all ages who find it difficult or impossible to read print resources, computers provide revolutionary access to information in electronic format. Library media specialists, educators, and parents can use these new resources to extend learning opportunities available for special needs students.

The main advantage of electronic text for the disabled and non-disabled population is that it can be easily altered and transformed to improve accessibility. Font size, style, and color can be efficiently customized to better meet the reading needs of a wider range of consumers. Web documents can also be quickly modified when they are copied and pasted into a word processor, such as *Microsoft Word 2000*. For example, an article from the Web that is pasted into a word processor could be made more readable for young students in different ways.

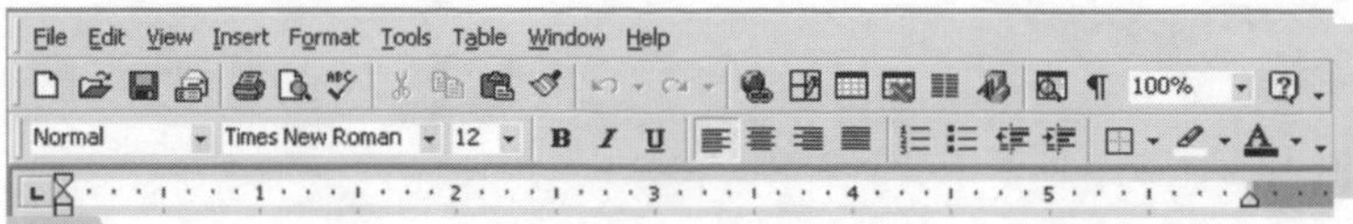

Figure 6.1: Microsoft Word Toolbar
[Screen shot reprinted by permission from Microsoft Corporation.]

The format option on the *MS Word* toolbar allows text spacing to be adjusted. After selecting the *format* heading, click on font. There is a tab to customize the appearance of the *font*, and a tab to adjust the spacing of the text. Young students may find expanded text easier to read, as there are fewer words in a line after text expansion has been performed. This method of simplifying a document can help

Font

Font | Character Spacing | Text Effects

Scale: 100%

Spacing: Normal   By:

Position: Normal   By:

Kerning for fonts: Points and above

Preview

Young students may find expanded text easier to read, as there

This is a TrueType font. This font will be used on both printer and screen.

Default...   OK   Cancel

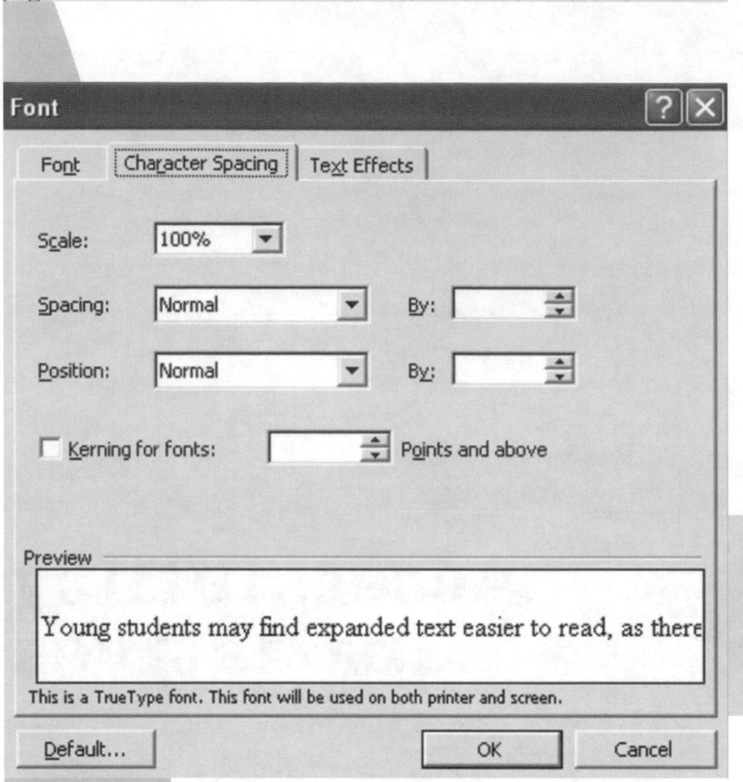

Figure 6.2: A view of the original Times New Roman text style and size selected for font and spacing customization in *Microsoft (MS) Word*. [Screen shot reprinted by permission from Microsoft Corporation.]

struggling learners who have difficulty reading more tightly spaced text.

Font

Font | Character Spacing | Text Effects

Font: Font style: Size:

Arial   Bold   18

Andale Mono IPA   Regular   14
Arial   Italic   16
Arial Black   Bold   18
Arial Narrow   Bold Italic   20
Arial Unicode MS   22

Font color: Underline style: Underline color:
Automatic   (none)   Automatic

Effects

Strikethrough   Shadow   Small caps
Double strikethrough   Outline   All caps
Superscript   Emboss   Hidden
Subscript   Engrave

Preview

Young students may find expand

This is a TrueType font. This font will be used on both printer and screen.

Default...   OK   Cancel

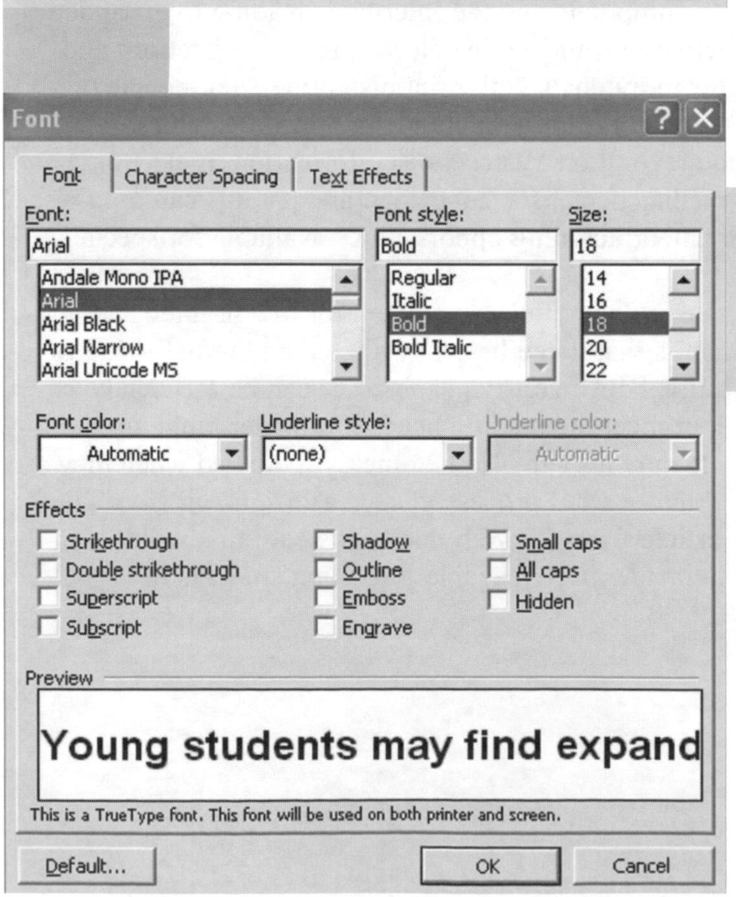

Figure 6.3: A preview of the text adjusted to bold Arial text and increased in size on the font adjustment window of *MS Word*. [Screen shot reprinted by permission from Microsoft Corporation.]

Web collections of eBooks are creating an ever-expanding electric library and improving access for everyone. Perhaps the most significant aspect of the growing availability of electronic information is that it offers greater independence for learners with disabilities. Instead of relying on another person to modify or read print resources, a person with a disability is now able to gain more

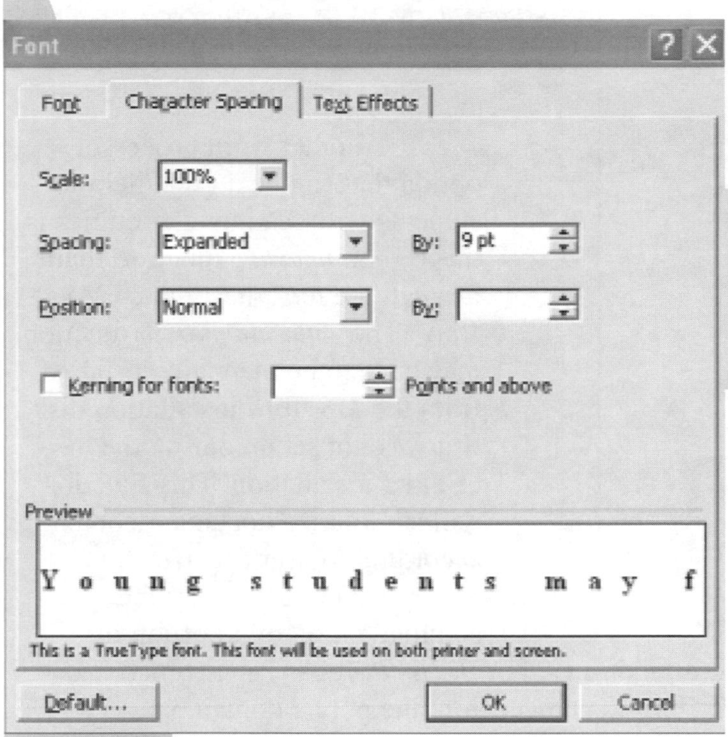

Figure 6.4: A view of the original text after the character spacing has been expanded using MS Word. [Screen shot reprinted by permission from Microsoft Corporation.]

control over his or her own learning through technology.

Electronic text accessed via text-to-speech software transforms the computer into a reading machine. This means that the computer users don't have to be able to see or read the text themselves as they review it. Some new text-to-speech products, such as *TextAloud MP3* <http://www.nextup.com> and *TextHELP! Read and Write Gold* <http://www.texthelp.com>, are also capable of converting electronic text to portable audio formats such as MP3 and Wav files. These technologies allow computer users to take documents from their computers and listen to the audio output on portable MP3 and CD players (see Chapter 13—Portable Technology Options).

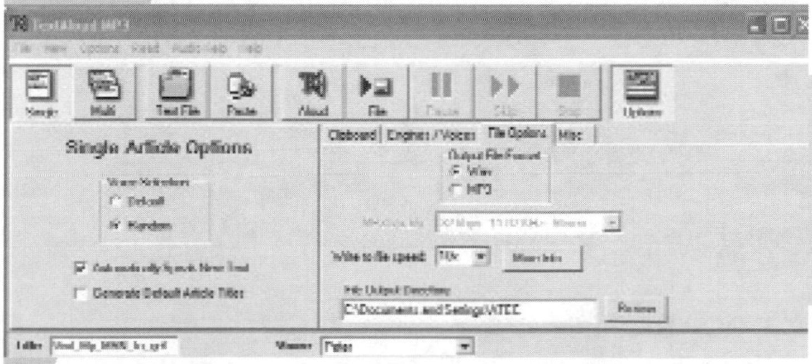

Figure 6.5: A view of the control panel of NextUp.com's TextAloud MP3 software showing the Wav and MP3 output file format options. [Reprinted with permission from NextUp.com <http://www.nextup.com>.]

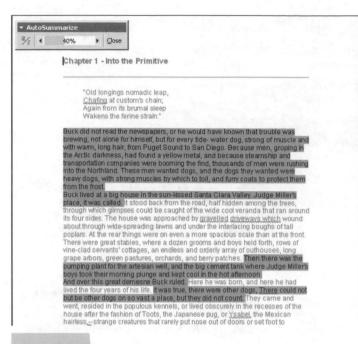

Figure 6.6: *AutoSummarize* **Feature of** *Microsoft Word* [Screen shot reprinted by permission from Microsoft Corporation.]

Another word processor option that can be a great help for students with reading difficulties is the *AutoSummarize* function found through the *tools* heading of *MS Word*. The *AutoSummarize* function may have to be manually installed from the *MS Word* installation disk if it was not set up during the original installation. This function will summarize document content according to user specifications.

Figure 6.6 shows the summarization of a portion of Chapter 1 of Jack London's *Call of the Wild*. It has been copied and pasted into an *MS Word* document from the public domain site Literature.org <http://www.literature.org>. The *AutoSummarize* function has been performed specifying a 40% summary. *AutoSummarize* options allow the computer user to view a highlighted summary and create a new summarized document.

These word processor options and functions provide convenient ways of modifying and presenting reading material for students with special needs. Older students can be taught to use these built-in assistive technologies to better address their own learning needs.

Online electronic text resources and services provide additional help for students who cannot work efficiently with print resources. Some of these initiatives are listed in this chapter. This is not a complete guide to all of the accessible resources on the Internet, but these listings spotlight some of the recent developments and exciting online projects. New projects and developments continue to emerge to enhance the delivery of accessible electronic fiction and nonfiction to people everywhere.

Bookshare.org

<http://www.bookshare.org>
Bookshare.org was launched in early 2002. It is a project of the Benetech Initiative, a nonprofit organization in Palo Alto, California. Bookshare.org is an online community that enables people with print

Figure 6.7: Bookshare.org [Reprinted with permission from Bookshare.org <http://www.bookshare.org>.]

disabilities (including visual impairments, learning disabilities, or mobility impairments) to share scanned books. A special exemption of the U.S. copyright law permits Bookshare.org to act as a clearinghouse for U.S. residents, who have a disability that affects reading, to legally download and share scanned books. Membership information and school service restrictions can be found through the Bookshare.org homepage.

Information for schools is available at <http://www.bookshare.org/web/MembersSchools.html>. There is a Web page of Bookshare.org reading materials recommended by K–12 teachers at <http://www.bookshare.org/web/TeacherRecommended1.html>. In February 2003, Bookshare.org and Pulse Data International, manufacturer of the BrailleNote family of Personal Data Assistants for persons who are blind, announced a collaborative effort that will allow BrailleNote users to download and read Bookshare.org books off-line.

Learn More About Bookshare.org

Interview with Alison Lingane, Senior Product Manager, Bookshare.org

Q. What is the background and inspiration for the development of the Bookshare.org service?

A. Bookshare.org is a project of a nonprofit organization, the Benetech Initiative, and was developed by Benetech. Bookshare.org builds on Benetech's 14-year history as a developer of adaptive technology, originally under the Arkenstone name. Having developed leading scanning and reading software for people with learning disabilities or visual impairments (*WYNN* and *OpenBook*), Benetech understands that there are large numbers of individuals (and schools) in the United States who regularly scan books to make them accessible. Bookshare.org was a logical extension of this work, since it enables those individuals and schools to share their scanning effort across the community, helping to build a centralized repository of scanned material that can be accessed by any qualifying individual in the country.

Q. Which consumer groups is the Bookshare.org service primarily directed at, and how are these groups being informed about this new resource?
A. Bookshare.org is directed at anybody in the United States who qualifies under the law for access (including people with learning disabilities, visual impairments, and mobility impairments) and has basic computer skills and an Internet connection. Our outreach efforts to date have included exhibiting and speaking at major conferences (of consumer disability groups, technology and disability, and for educators), through our monthly announce only e-Newsletter (to subscribe, send a blank e-mail to <Bookshare.org-discuss-subscribe@topica .com>, and through articles in relevant publications. Our school pilot projects are also a way for us to raise awareness about Bookshare.org while receiving very direct feedback from school-based users.

Q. How could K–12, postsecondary, and community libraries extend their services through Bookshare.org?
A. For schools, by sponsoring subscriptions for their students, either on an individual basis or by taking advantage of our no-cost account-management services <http://www.bookshare.org/web/AboutOrgani zations.html>. For libraries, by pointing patrons to the public domain material and educating them about the availability of the copyrighted books with a subscription. For libraries, we would also permit them to install the talking book reader software on their PCs, enabling free access for library patrons to public domain material, or for subscribers who may not have PC or Internet access available elsewhere.

Q. To what extent are schools currently using the Bookshare.org service?
A. Schools are increasingly turning to Bookshare.org as a resource for students. About 25% of our current members are under 18.

Q. Are there many K–12 curriculum materials available through Bookshare.org? Is expanded access to K–12 curriculum materials one of the goals of Bookshare.org?
A. Bookshare.org has a growing collection of K–12 recommended reading material, viewable at this link: <http://www.bookshare.org/ web/TeacherRecommended1.html>. We are working with several schools on pilot projects and plan to add upwards of 200 additional books to this listing, based on requests from our school pilot sites and targeted state department of education reading lists over the next six months. We hope also to involve more schools that are scanning and proofreading books for their students to enable those books to be shared across the community.

Center for Applied Special Technology (CAST)

<http://www.cast.org>
CAST is a not-for-profit organization that was founded in 1984. CAST receives funding for research and various initiatives through government agencies, corporations, organizations, and private donors. Among the many resources that can be found through the CAST site are the CAST eText Spider and the CAST Universal Learning Center <http://ulc.cast.org>.

eText Spider is an online tool that is capable of searching multiple sites, through a single query, to locate public domain materials in various online libraries, including Project Gutenberg. eText Spider provides an efficient way for students and educators to search for electronic resources without having to visit a number of Web sites.

The Universal Learning Center (ULC) is a newly created directory and repository of K–12 digital curriculum materials. ULC is a subscription-based service that was limited to selected U.S. school sites during the 2002–2003 school year. For current membership information, contact ULC at <ulchelp@cast.org>.

Recording for the Blind & Dyslexic

<http://www.rfbd.org>
On September 3, 2002, Recording for the Blind & Dyslexic (RFB&D) released its inaugural collection of over 6,000 digitally recorded education titles on CD. RFB&D's AudioPlus™ digitally recorded textbooks provide instant navigation and bookmarking capabilities for pages, subheadings, and chapters. A single CD can hold the contents of an entire textbook, which would normally have to be recorded on multiple cassettes. These portable features increase independence while reducing the need for students to carry and sort through numerous tapes. Membership information is available through <http://www.rfbd.org/membership.htm>.

Project Gutenberg eText Library

<http://www.gutenberg.net>
For over 30 years, hundreds of volunteers have been involved in digitally re-publishing books through Project Gutenberg. Literary works that were first published with proper copyright notice at least 75 years

ago are considered to be part of the public domain. (There are variations to this copyright rule that are explained on the project's "public domain and copyright how-to page.") Over 6,200 copyright cleared eBooks have now been published on the Web through Project Gutenberg.

The Project Gutenberg eText Library June 2002 Edition (four-CD Set) can be purchased through Technology Associates, Inc., <http://www.techass.com/guten/>. Twenty percent of the profits of the sales of these Windows and Linux compatible CDs go to support Project Gutenberg. The four-volume set includes a searchable index for over 5,000 eText documents on the CDs that have been compiled by Project Gutenberg from 1971 to June 2002.

AssistiveMedia.org

<http://www.assistivemedia.org>
AssistiveMedia.org, or AM, was launched for computer users in 1998. AM focuses on producing spoken-word recordings of copyright-approved material from reputable periodicals. This site is designed to serve the needs of mature consumers with vision or reading disabilities. This is a free service that requires the installation of *RealPlayer* from *RealNetworks* to access the recorded materials. This utility can be downloaded for free through the AssistiveMedia.org Web site.

American Foundation for the Blind (AFB)

<http://www.afb.org>
The American Foundation for the blind offers services and extensive information on its Web site. Agencies in the United States and Canada providing Braille, large print, and audio production services can be found through the "Directory of Services" link on the AFB homepage.

Canadian National Institute for the Blind (CNIB)

<http://www.cnib.ca>
The CNIB site lists many resources including the CNIB library program for libraries and schools <http://www.cnib.ca/library/libraries_schools/index.htm>.

► International Children's Digital Library

<http://www.icdlbooks.org>
Access to children's books in a variety of languages through this new service currently requires a high-end computer with a high-speed Internet connection. However, a new version of this service, planned for commencement in the summer of 2003, will provide access to any Internet-connected computer.

► National Center for Accessible Media (NCAM)

<http://ncam.wgbh.org>
The mission of NCAM is to expand access to present and future media for people with disabilities. NCAM has developed a captioning and audio description authoring tool for developers of Web and CD-ROM-based multimedia. MAGpie 2.01 beta is a Java™ application that runs on Windows 9x/NT/2000/XP and on Mac OSX. This product can be downloaded from the NCAM site <http://ncam.wgbh.org/webaccess/magpie/index.html#magpie2>.

More information on past and present NCAM projects and resources can be found through its homepage. (Additional information on captioning is discussed in Chapter 12.)

► Private Services

Some private initiatives are providing very good online resources. The Starfall.com site <http://www.starfall.com> provides interactive books and games for K–2 reading development. Starfall.com also makes available free, downloadable print resources for these online books. Older students can find excellent electronic text resources through other sites such as PinkMonkey.com <http://www.pinkmonkey.com> and SparkNotes.com <http://www.sparknotes.com>.

Numerous companies provide eBook services and other forms of accessible literature, such as books on cassette, CD, and video. These businesses range from small individually operated services to large companies such as Amazon.com. Find them on the Web through keyword searches for eBooks, audio books, or related headings on Internet search engines.

eBooks, and Books on Tape and CD

Amazon.com <http://www.amazon.com/eBooks>

Audible.com <http://www.audible.com>

Audio Book Club <http://www.audiobookclub.com>

Audio Books on Compact Disk, Inc. <http://www.abcdinc.com/>

Barnes & Noble <http://eBooks.barnesandnoble.com>

Blackstone Audio Books <http://www.blackstoneaudio.com/>

Books On Tape <http://www.booksontape.com>

Chapters.Indigo.ca <http://www.chapters.indigo.ca/> (Browse under Audiobooks)

eBooks.com <http://www.eBooks.com>

KidsReads.com <http://www.kidsreads.com/features/0529-audio.asp>

Talking Book World <http://www.talkingbooks.com/>

Time Warner AudioBooks <http://www.twbookmark.com/audiobooks/index.html>

Walmart.com <http://www.walmart.com> (Browse for audiobooks under Books)

*See Appendix A for a list of free online eText resources.

Chapter 7

Library Accessibility Needs

A good way to evaluate the accessibility of your school library media center is to take a tour of it. Perhaps you've worked in your library setting for years, but have you spent a day in your library media center while in a wheelchair, on crutches, or without your vision? Investigative role-playing can be an effective way of raising student and staff accessibility awareness. Invite students and staff to brainstorm different ways of simulating disability experiences in the school or library setting. After participants spend time in the library media center under these circumstances, invite feedback on the ways it could be made more accessible. Special educators, students, and staff with disabilities can provide leadership for these types of exercises. Some Web sites to explore for disability simulation ideas include:

- Hearing loss simulation <http://filebox.vt.edu/users/romille6/Projects/DisabilitySimulation.htm>
- WebAIM's online low vision disability simulation <http://www.webaim.org/simulations/lowvision>
- WebAIM's online cognitive disability simulation <http://www.webaim.org/simulations/cognitive>
- WebAIM's online screen reader simulation <http://www.webaim.org/simulations/screenreader>
- Disability Simulation Race 2002 <http://www.auburn.edu/ada/disability_simulation_race_2002.html>

- Simulation experience, physical disabilities <http://www.coe.ilstu.edu/jpbakke/sed411/physical%20disability%20simulation.htm>
- Avoca West School, fifth-grade disability simulation pictures <http://www.avoca.k12.il.us/fifthgrade/diffphotos.html>
- Zimmerman Low Vision Simulation Kit <http://www.spedex.com/zimmerman-lvsk/text/index.htm>

As well as promoting school involvement in the library media center assessment process, consider inviting community disability and advocacy groups for a visit. Listen to their feedback and take note of what you hear. Some jurisdictions provide library assessment services. The LIFE (Library Inclusion For Everyone) Project in Connecticut is a collaborative project involving the University of Connecticut's A.J. Pappanikou Center for Developmental Disabilities, the State of Connecticut Office of Protection and Advocacy for Persons with Disabilities, and the Connecticut State Library. LIFE provides information and technical assistance to librarians in Connecticut to make services and programs welcoming to all. This model could be adopted to assist K–12 library media specialists as well. For more information on the LIFE Project, visit its Web site <http://www.uconnced.org/life/lifehome.htm>.

When a specialized consulting service such as LIFE is not available, school district library media specialists and special educators can work together on professional development days to tour library media centers within their zones or districts. Construct a checklist or note-taking system to record the evaluation team's observations. A multidisciplinary team or committee could consider and prioritize recommendations on library accessibility. There may be common issues in different schools that could be reviewed and researched by committee members. Existing library accessibility checklists, such as the ones listed in the following section on facilities, could be used to provide focus for this work.

Facilities

Guidelines and checklists have been developed to assist planners and library personnel with facility accessibility issues.

- The *UFAS Accessibility Checklist* is a workbook that enables people to survey buildings for compliance with the Uniform Federal Accessibility Standards (UFAS). This online document has a special form for libraries <http://www.ada-infonet.org/documents/architectural-documents/ufas-main.asp>.
- *The Americans with Disabilities Act (ADA) Checklist for Readily Achievable Barrier Removal* is available online <http://www.usdoj

.gov/crt/ada/checktxt.htm>.

- *The ADA Accessibility Guidelines for Buildings and Facilities (ADAAG)*, as amended through January 1998, is available online <http://www.access-board.gov/adaag/html/adaag.htm>. Section 8 of this online document covers library specifications for general accessibility, reading and studying areas, check-out areas, card catalogs and magazine displays, and stacks.
- The University of Washington's DO-IT Web site includes a page, Universal Access to Libraries <http://www.washington.edu/doit/ UA/>, with a collection of resources on library accessibility. *Universal Access: Making Library Resources Accessible to People with Disabilities* <http://www.washington.edu/doit/ Brochures/ Technology/libsrv.html> includes checklist questions to guide decision making on library accessibility issues.
- *Starting Points: An Introduction to Creating Access in Community-Based Organizations* is an online companion resource to the Alliance for Technology Access publication, "Access Aware: Extending your reach to People with Disabilities." *Starting Points* provides a collection of self-assessments that organizations can use to start examining their communications, facilities, programs, technology, and Web sites <http://www.ataccess.org/resources/ acaw/startingpoints.html>.
- The *Checklists for Making Library Automation Accessible to Disabled Patrons* document is available online <http://www.trace .wisc.edu/docs/accessible_library/library.htm>.
- *Canadian Guidelines on Library and Information Services for People with Disabilities* is an online document available through the Canadian Library Association <http://www.cla.ca/about/ disabils.htm>.

Workstation Characteristics

Book check-out and library administration workstations should be evaluated to ensure that library users in wheelchairs are visible to staff. If counters are too high or there are structures and objects that obstruct the view from the check-out area, students in wheelchairs will find it more difficult to get assistance. Counters that are too high also make it difficult for persons in wheelchairs to share and reach information that allows them to help themselves. There should be access to one or more modified or adjustable computer workstations to accommodate the needs of people who cannot access a standard computer desk. More information on wheelchair accessible furniture is reviewed in Chapter 10.

The Multiple-Disability Workstation for Small Libraries (Banks, D., Noble, S., 1997), a paper delivered at the 1997 California State

University, Northridge (CSUN) Technology and Persons with Disabilities Conference, reviews workstation considerations for various disability groups <http://www.rit.edu/%7Eeasi/itd/itdv04n1/article1.html>.

Seating

Look into different styles of seating and seating arrangements. Greater comfort options make the library media center a more welcoming environment. Modular furniture offers flexibility, allowing staff to arrange seating in different ways. The ability to adjust and experiment with different seating options makes it easier to transform areas of the library. Some companies that sell library furniture have designed Web sites that display various styles of chairs, benches, and tables. August Inc. has examples of modular seating systems for libraries on its Web site <http://www.augustinc.com/profiles/library.htm>.

Lighting

Is the lighting in your library media center adequate and consistent? If there are no sources of natural light, check on the lighting levels in different areas, seminar rooms, divided cubicles, and study areas. If there is natural lighting, evaluate whether excessive glare interferes with the ability of students to work at various seating areas, or to view computer or television monitors. If the library media center is in use during the evenings, compare the lighting levels during daytime and nighttime hours.

Materials

Look at the types of learning materials available in the library media center. Are the materials suitable for a range of abilities and interests? Are key resources available in more than one format? Can specialized materials be requested, shared, or rotated between schools to provide access to a wider selection of learning resources?

Selection

A variety of formats should be available to or included in the inclusive library media center collection. Some suggestions include:

- Large print materials
- Video resources
- Books on tape
- Books on CD
- High interest/low difficulty reading selections
- Tactile/Braille materials
- Modified literature resources (study guides and notes)

- Talking book sets or multimedia editions of novels
- Interactive materials

Accessibility

On November 15, 2002, the U.S. Department of Education announced that it had awarded $199,911 to the National Center on Accessing the General Curriculum (NCAC) at the Center for Applied Special Technology (CAST) in Wakefield, Massachusetts, to develop a voluntary national file format for the electronic transmission of instructional materials for students who are blind and students with other disabilities. This new project is intended to improve access to the general education curriculum for students with disabilities. Agreement on a standardized file format will assist various groups interested in providing accessible instructional materials to states, schools, educators, and students who are blind or print disabled and in need of textbooks in Braille or other alternative formats. More information on the National File Format Initiative (NFF) can be found online <http://www.cast.org/ncac/>.

Guidelines for Accessing Alternative Format Educational Materials are outlined in an online document prepared by Barbara Nail-Chiwetalu <http://www.loc.gov/nls/guidelines.htm>. This document points out that there are variable state systems by which alternative format materials may be accessed.

Technology

Library media centers can offer students a wide range of hardware, software, and portable devices. The accessibility of these technologies, along with Internet connectivity, provides students with new learning options.

Mouse, Keyboard, Screen

Computer access devices will be discussed in more detail in Chapter 10. However, library media specialists should evaluate the alternatives they are currently providing for computer access within their library media centers. If just one type of mouse, keyboard, or screen is available, staff should become more familiar with the wider variety of input and output hardware options available for computers. Usability is enhanced when a variety of computer access hardware is available to students.

Software

If all of your library media center computers are running the Windows operating system, then all of your software choices will have to be compatible with the versions of Windows installed on these computers. Familiarize yourself with software choices that are available for the

Windows, Mac, and UNIX/Linux operating systems. You may find that you can offer a greater selection to students and staff if your library media center has one or more workstations with alternative operating systems.

Time Limits

Set realistic goals by taking into account the amount of time you and your staff have to learn about new technologies and software. Unless you have an unlimited budget, time, and experienced personnel to guide you, you should not expect to transform an inaccessible library media center overnight. Creating an accessible library media center is a process that could take years and will really be an ongoing project. Spend time learning and planning before buying.

Students also need time to learn about and become skilled in using new technologies. This becomes a problem when many students depend on computers or other limited resources. Keep in mind that students with different learning needs will require varying amounts of time to access materials and make use of them. Skillfully managing students who need additional time with high-demand resources will be a challenge for library media specialists. Communicate with the teachers of these students to determine the best ways to fairly allocate the library media center's technology resources.

Personnel

In life, there is always more to learn. This is certainly true when it comes to the field of disability awareness. Even professionals who work full time in disability-related occupations are on a never-ending quest to learn more. One's level of disability awareness often depends on past disability-related experiences. For educators who have had personal interaction with friends, relatives, colleagues, and students with disabilities, the level of awareness will be greater than for a teacher who has had few interactions with people with disabilities. Real-life experiences are excellent teachers, but other resources can help to educate library media center personnel and the school community. The National Information Center for Children and Youth with Disabilities (NICHCY) has compiled a list of disability awareness resources available through various organizations <http://www.nichcy.org/pubs/bibliog/bib13txt.htm>.

Attitudes

Attitudes toward disability are demonstrated through behavior, language, policies, and the overall learning environment. Some disability-awareness trainers emphasize that the humanly imposed and physical constraints of an environment can serve to disable a person. That way of looking at the learning environment creates a new kind of awareness in the school setting. Educators who consciously look for barriers and identify obstacles to learning for students with special needs become environmental problem solvers. Remember that sometimes small changes can make a very big difference.

Communicating

Sensitivity to the language that is used to address disability concerns and people with disabilities is an issue for consideration. Some expressions and terminology that were routinely used in the past are no longer considered to be appropriate. The "person first" style of language has been embraced by many organizations. Some examples of person first language are listed:

- "People with disabilities" instead of "the handicapped or the disabled."
- "My son has autism" instead of "my son is autistic."
- "He has a learning disability" instead of "he's learning disabled."

More examples of person first language can be found on several sites on the Internet. The Texas Council for Developmental Disabilities has a useful link with more examples <http://www.txddc.state.tx.us/publications/textpfangback.asp>.

Accessibility

In the mind of the student with a disability, how accessible is your library media center staff? This may be a question of how comfortable the student is in seeking assistance from library media center personnel. Some students with disabilities are very strong advocates for themselves, while others are shy about speaking up and requesting assistance. Do library media center staff members initiate contact with these students on a regular basis to get to know the students and show that they are available to assist? How do staff members react when students approach them for help? Does the student feel that his or her request is welcomed, or does he or she get the impression that he or she is imposing on the staff? Library media center personnel can find out how they can work well with students with disabilities by seeking their advice. Provide students with information on the best times to get individual assistance in the library media center if low staffing levels and workloads are factors. Conducting student interviews or focus groups that involve special needs students are a couple of ways to gather input about library media center services.

Professional Development

Fact sheet and tutorial resources help staff provide quick information about accommodations for students with disabilities. The following quick reference resources can be found on the Internet:

- The JAN (Job Accommodation Network) Accommodation Fact Sheet Series includes reference sheets for educational settings <http://janweb.icdi.wvu.edu/media/fact.html>.
- The Lighthouse International site has a page called "Getting the Facts—For Free!" <http://publications.lighthouse.org/publications/catalog/free_facts.cfm>.
- Adaptive Technology Tutorial Resources are available through the University of Toronto's Special Needs Opportunity Window (SNOW) site <http://snow.utoronto.ca/technology/tutorials/index.html>.

Learn More

Technology and the Need for Collaboration

Sheryl Burgstahler, Ph.D., administrator and affiliate associate professor at the University of Washington (UW), is the director of project DO-IT (Disabilities, Opportunities, Internetworking, and Technology). The goal of DO-IT is to maximize the participation, progress, academic achievement, and career advancement of students with disabilities through the use of computers, adaptive technology, and the Internet.

Among Burgstahler's many published works on the topics of education, technology, and disabilities is a white paper developed in 2002 for the Postsecondary Outcomes Network of the National Center on Secondary Education and Transition (NCSET). It can be found online <http://www.ncset.hawaii.edu/Publications/Pdfs/role_of_technology.pdf>.

The Role of Technology in Preparing Youth with Disabilities for Postsecondary Education and Employment examines important issues related to the roles of technology for students with disabilities. Topics discussed in this paper include accommodation versus universal design, peer and mentor support, legislation, and policy. Lack of educator training, funding, and insufficient consideration of the needs of disabled students when purchasing educational technology are identified as some of the barriers that prevent students with disabilities from gaining access to enabling technology that could allow them to reach their full learning and career potential.

Technology has the potential to improve the educational and career outcomes for people with disabilities. However, Burgstahler's paper suggests that this potential will not be realized unless barriers to reaching the following goals are overcome.

In another article, *Distance Learning: The Library's Role in Ensuring Access to Everyone (Library Hi Tech*, Volume 20, #4, 2002,), Burgstahler describes the role that libraries can play in assuring that all distance learning students and instructors have access to the electronic resources they offer. She suggests that libraries take the following steps to assure the accessibility of their online services.

- Develop a policy statement about the library's commitment to accessibility.
- Adopt guidelines for accessible electronic and information technology (e.g., those developed for the federal government in response to Section 508 of the Rehabilitation Act).
- Fix simple errors (the vast majority of accessibility mistakes in Web pages) in existing products immediately.
- Establish evaluation criteria and an evaluation process and then regularly evaluate progress toward accessibility goals
- Disseminate accessibility policy, guidelines, and procedures throughout the library.
- Provide training and support.
- Develop procedures for responding quickly to requests for disability-related accommodations.
- Procure accessible products.

These recommendations can be used to help libraries develop policies, guidelines, and procedures for making their electronic resources accessible to people with disabilities. Library staff should also encourage patrons to inform them when their resources are not accessible. They should encourage their professional organizations to take a leadership role in promoting the development of accessible libraries. Distance learning programs, colleges and universities, and state governments should also be encouraged to promote the accessibility of electronic and information technology.

Burgstahler suggests that it will take multi-level collaboration to meet the technology needs of students with disabilities. "Institutions tend to focus on the services they provide within their own facility, not those that individuals might encounter as they move through life's transitions. DO-IT is an example of a program that helps students with disabilities while they are still in high school and continues to work with them through postsecondary education and careers. DO-IT provides participants with technology and fills in the gap in transition services from K–12 to postsecondary to employment. Unfortunately, few students with disabilities have access to the type of resource DO-IT offers. More work in this area is needed, starting with a regular dialogue between stakeholders at both the K–12 and postsecondary levels. Those who help select technology for students at the precollege level should consider how well that technology will serve the student at the postsecondary level; similarly, those who provide technology to postsecondary students with disabilities should help students consider the technology that will serve them best in employment."

More information about professional development is covered in Chapter 15. Library media specialists may want to consider the acquisition of educational materials related to disability issues and assistive technology. ORCCA Technology, Inc., <http://www.orcca.com> has produced three interactive multimedia CD-ROM products that help people to learn more about assistive technology <http://www.orcca.com/MMProd.htm>:

- *Forrest Center Stage* (an interactive storybook that allows children and adults to learn about assistive technology).
- *The GATE—Guide to Assistive Technology Experiences* (an awareness and training resource that reviews six age groups of assistive technology users).
- *The Assistive Technology Exploration and Training Center—Adaptive Computer Technology Room* (a new interactive CD-ROM that lets you explore a virtual Assistive Technology Center; you can learn about the features of devices and software for adaptive computer input and output, find out where to obtain them, view them in typical applications, and try them out by interacting with simulations).

Figure 7.1: Computer Lab *Assistive Technology Exploration and Training Center—Adaptive Computer Technology Room* [Reprinted with permission from ORCCA Technology, Inc. <http://www.orcca.com>.]

References

Banks, Dick and Noble, Steve, *The Multiple-Disability Workstation for Small Libraries*, paper delivered at the California State University Northridge Conference, March 1997 <http://www.rit.edu/%7Eeasi/itd/itdv04n1/article1.html>.

Burgstahler, Sheryl, *Distance Learning: The Library's Role in Ensuring Access to Everyone, Library Hi Tech*, Volume 20, #4, pp. 420–432, 2002 <http://rudolfo.emeraldinsight.com/vl=6682964/cl=122/nw=1/rpsv/cw/www/mcb/07378831/v20n4/contp1-1.htm>.

Burgstahler, Sheryl, *The Role of Technology in Preparing Youth with Disabilities for Postsecondary Education and Employment*, White Paper developed for the Postsecondary Outcomes Network of the National Center on Secondary Education and Transition (NCSET), 2002 <http://www.ncset.hawaii.edu/Publications/Pdfs/role_of_technology.pdf>.

Canadian Guidelines on Library and Information Services for People with Disabilities, Canadian Library Association, February 1997 <http://www.cla.ca/about/disabils.htm>.

Disability Awareness Kit—A Training Resource for Public Library Customer Service Staff, State Library of Victoria, Australia <http://openroad.net.au/access/dakit>.

Morales, Tom, et al, *Starting Points: An Introduction to Creating Access in Community-Based Organizations*, Alliance for Technology Access, 2002 <http://www.ataccess.org/resources/acaw/startingpoints.html>.

Nail-Chiwetalu, Barbara, *Guidelines for Accessing Alternative Format Educational Materials*, National Library Service, March 1, 2000 <http://lcweb.loc.gov/nls/other/guidelines.html>.

Universal Access: Making Library Resources Accessible to People with Disabilities, University of Washington, DO-IT <http://www.washington.edu/doit/Brochures/Technology/libsrv.html>.

Voluntary National Standard for Accessible Digital Instructional Materials to be Developed, November 15, 2002, Press Release, United States Department of Education <http://www.ed.gov/PressReleases/11-2002/11152002a.html>.

Chapter 8

Built-In Computer System Accessibility Features

The operating system (OS) is the most important software that runs on a computer. It provides access to other application programs and performs basic tasks such as recognizing input from the keyboard or alternative input devices and sending output to the display screen. The operating system keeps track of files and directories on the disk and controls peripheral devices such as scanners and printers.

The choice of operating system determines, to a great extent, the applications that can be run on a computer. Microsoft's Windows and Apple's Macintosh systems are examples of popular desktop operating systems. These and other operating systems continue to evolve through upgraded versions that come with new and more advanced user features.

OS developers haven't ignored the need for access features to assist computer users with disabilities. In recent years, more specialized accessibility features for computer users with disabilities have been added to operating systems largely due to U.S. federal legislative amendments to the Rehabilitation Act.

On August 7, 1998, President Clinton signed into law the *Workforce Investment Act*, including Rehabilitation Act amendments to expand and strengthen Section 508. This amendment requires that U.S. federal agencies and departments ensure that electronic and information technology be accessible to federal employees and members of the public with disabilities. Section 508 demands that all federal departments and agencies, including the U.S. Postal Service and contractors providing services and products to federal agencies, provide Section 508 compliant deliverables. This requirement must be met unless doing so would place an undue burden on a department or agency. Section 508 addresses accessibility for people who have visual, hearing, or motor disabilities.

As a result, new technologies purchased by the U.S. government must comply with Section 508 technical standards. These standards are organized into six sections: *Software Applications and Operating Systems; Web-based Intranet and Internet Information and Applications; Telecommunications Products; Video and Multimedia Products; Self Contained, Closed Products; Desktop and Portable Computers*. These measures have been implemented to provide improved access to government information to the estimated 54 million Americans who live with some level of disability.

The enforcement of Section 508 began on June 21, 2001. Although the binding technology standards only apply to the U.S. government and not the private sector, technology manufacturers hoping to sell hardware and software to the government must ensure their products are Section 508 compliant. Manufacturers are not required to modify their products, but federal departments and agencies are required to give priority to procuring products that comply with Section 508. Manufacturers have responded to the urgency of this legislation. More products are being designed with accessibility features that comply with Section 508 in order to be successfully marketed to the U.S. government. As a result, improved accessibility features on new computer operating systems are providing benefits to users around the world. To learn more about this legislation, review the series of online lessons on Section 508 awareness <http://www.section508.gov/508Awareness/html/Lessons.html>.

Since developers are now including more accessibility features in widely used operating systems, it is important to be aware of the built-in options that are available. Many computer users accept the default settings on the computers they use without realizing that the systems can be configured for people with different accessibility needs. Built-in accessibility features can help people who have disabilities to work more enjoyably and productively. Knowledge of these features may also reduce expenditures for unnecessary add-on assistive technologies.

▶ Windows

Microsoft has an extensive collection of accessibility resources available through its Microsoft Accessibility homepage <http://www.microsoft.com/enable/>. The site is well designed to assist educators wanting to provide accessibility options that help students with disabilities work more productively. There are a variety of ways to find information through the site, whether it is disability specific, a general overview, or a comparison of the features available on Windows.

Figure 8.1: Microsoft Accessibility Homepage [Screen shot reprinted with permission from Microsoft Corporation <http://www.microsoft.com/enable/>.]

The *Step by Step Tutorials* are a great way to find out about the accessibility features available for Windows operating systems as well as other Microsoft software. Microsoft grants permission for educational institutions to reprint its *Step by Step Tutorials* for educational purposes only. Review the reprint guidelines at <http://www.microsoft.com/enable/training/default.htm>.

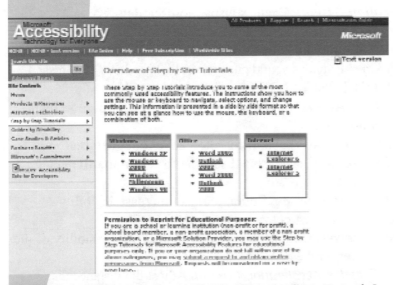

Figure 8.2: Microsoft Accessibility Step by Step Tutorials [Screen shot reprinted with permission from Microsoft Corporation <http://www.microsoft.com/enable/training/default.aspx>.]

If you want to customize the operating system settings for a specific disability, visit the *Guides by Disability* page. It contains detailed resources for visual, hearing, mobility, language, and learning impairments.

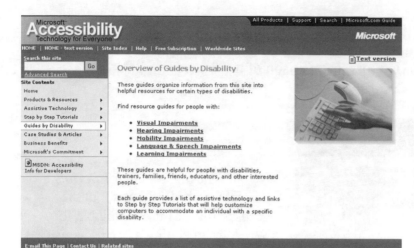

A comparison chart of the accessibility features available in the different versions of Microsoft Windows, with hyperlinks to *Step By Step* guides, can be found at <http://www.microsoft.com/enable/Products/chartwindows.aspx>.

Figure 8.3: Microsoft Accessibility Guides by Disability
[Screen shot reprinted by permission from Microsoft Corporation <http://www.microsoft.com/enable/guides/default.aspx.>]

Windows hearing features include:
- *SoundSentry*: Provides a visual warning for system sounds
- *ShowSounds*: Displays captions for computer system speech and sounds
- *SerialKeys*: Provides support for alternative input devices
- *Chat, NetMeeting, Windows Messenger*: Text-based communication
- *Sound Volume Control*: Adjust for hearing impairment or noisy environment
- *Notification (visual)*: Enables visual notifications

Windows vision features include:
- *ToggleKeys*: Provides sound cues when locking keys are pressed (CAPS LOCK, NUM LOCK, or SCROLL LOCK)
- *MouseKeys*: Allows use of numeric keypad to control movement of the mouse pointer
- *SerialKeys*: Provides support for alternative input devices
- *Sound Schemes*: Select a sound scheme to assign to different program events
- *High Contrast Schemes*: Option that can increase legibility through high contrast color and adjusted font size
- *Pointer Schemes*: Options designed to increase the visibility of the mouse pointer on the computer screen
- *Pointer Speed & Acceleration/Control*: Adjust the distance that the pointer moves in relation to the distance the mouse or trackball moves
- *Pointer Visibility*: Options to show pointer trails, hide pointer while typing, give pointer location cue
- *ClickLock*: Highlight or drag without having to hold down the mouse button

- *SnapTo*: Moves the pointer to the default button of a dialog box (useful when the narrator function is enabled)
- *Magnifier*: Displays a magnified portion of the computer screen
- *Narrator*: A text-to-speech utility that reads what is displayed on the computer screen
- *Cursor Width Control*: Adjusts cursor width and blink rate
- *Use/Disable Personalized Menus*: The feature that automatically updates and lists, at the top of the menu, items that are used most often; this feature can be disabled if it does not meet a user's accessibility needs
- *Notification (sound)*: Gives sound notification when an accessibility feature is turned on or off

Windows mobility features include:
- *StickyKeys*: This function helps people who have difficulty holding down more that one key at the same time
- *FilterKeys*: Helps users avoid typing difficulties from brief or repeated keystrokes; it can be used to slow down the repeat rate
- *MouseKeys*: Allows use of numeric keypad to control movement of the mouse pointer
- *SerialKeys*: Provides support for alternative input devices
- *ToggleKeys*: Provides sound cues when locking keys are pressed (CAPS LOCK, NUM LOCK, or SCROLL LOCK)
- *Pointer Schemes*: Options designed to increase the visibility of the mouse pointer on the computer screen
- *Pointer Speed & Acceleration*: Adjust the distance that the pointer moves in relation to the distance the mouse or trackball moves
- *Pointer Visibility*: Options to show pointer trails, hide pointer while typing, give pointer location cue
- *SnapTo*: Moves the pointer to the default button of a dialog box (useful when the narrator function is enabled)
- *Mouse configuration for right or left hand use*: Choose right-handed or left-handed mouse button configuration
- *ClickLock*: Highlight or drag without having to hold down the mouse button
- *Onscreen Keyboard*: A utility that displays a virtual keyboard on the computer screen, allowing people with mobility impairments to enter data by using a pointing device or joystick
- *Cursor Width Control*: Adjusts cursor width and blink rate

Windows language and learning features include:
- *Pointer Schemes*: Options designed to increase the visibility of the mouse pointer on the computer screen
- *SerialKeys*: Provides support for alternative input devices
- *Pointer Speed & Acceleration*: Adjust the distance that the pointer moves in relation to the distance the mouse or trackball moves

- *Pointer Visibility*: Options to show pointer trails, hide pointer while typing, give pointer location cue
- *ClickLock*: Highlight or drag without having to hold down the mouse button
- *SnapTo*: Moves the pointer to the default button of a dialog box (useful when the narrator function is enabled)
- *Cursor Width Control*: Adjusts cursor width and blink rate
- *Use/Disable Personalized Menus*: The feature that automatically updates and lists, at the top of the menu, items that are used most often; this feature can be disabled if it does not meet a user's accessibility needs

Windows seizure disorder features include:
- *Cursor Blink Rate*: The cursor blink rate can be adjusted or set to None to turn blinking off completely to meet the needs of people with seizure disorders triggered by flashing or blinking objects

Macintosh

Apple's Web site has a well-organized collection of accessibility resources to help users easily find information about built-in operating system accessibility features and compatible add-on assistive technologies that can be purchased through other companies.

At the Apple Special Needs Web page <http://www.apple.com/disability/>, consumers can look for disability solutions according to categories displayed for:

- Vision
- Hearing
- Physical/Motor
- Literacy & Learning
- Language & Communication

Each category button links to information explaining the disability-specific accessibility solutions the system includes. There are further links to other resources that may be helpful to address a person's needs.

Apple introduced its Universal Access system with the Mac OS X version 10.1 operating system. The Universal Access system allows users to easily configure their computer systems for customized support. Users can enable full keyboard access, sticky keys, repeat key rate, and mouse keys. Other accessibility features of this system include speakable items, text-to-speech, and resizable high-resolution icons. Details about Apple's compliance with Section 508 accessibility standards are reviewed on Apple's Federal Compliance Web page <http://www.apple.com/federal/compliance/>.

The Mac OS X is a rebuilt implementation of the Macintosh operating system. It is an innovative development in that the foundation of its architecture is an open source, UNIX-based core called Darwin <http://developer.apple.com/darwin/>. Built into this system are technologies that aid seeing, hearing, and using the keyboard and mouse.

Apple's Mac OS X (version 10.2 and higher) has accessibility features that go beyond the federal government's Section 508 accessibility statute requirements. For users with visual impairments, a zoom option is available to magnify the contents of the screen. Users can also select the white text on black background contrast feature as a viewing and reading option. The system can read text and speak alerts, providing auditory support for users. People with hearing impairments can configure the system for screen flashing alerts instead of auditory signals. Mouse control and keyboard navigation options are also available for users with mobility challenges. The OS X Jaguar Universal Access Web page <http://www.apple.com/macosx/features/universalaccess.html> provides more information about the accessibility features of this system.

Earlier versions of the Macintosh operating system (7.x, 8.x, 9.x) also have built-in or downloadable accessibility features available. The *CloseView* utility provides options for users with visual disabilities, while *Easy Access* system functions (MouseKeys, Sticky Keys, Slow Keys, Text-To-Speech), speakable items, and talking and visual alerts are also included as accessibility options. Visit the Apple Special Needs Accessibility Web page <http://www.apple.com/disability/easyaccess .html> to review and download these features.

If you want to save time searching for assistive technologies that are compatible with Macintosh operating systems, visit the Macintosh Products Guide—Assistive Technologies Web page <http://guide.apple.com/uscategories/assisttech.lasso>. Enter specific search criteria to find appropriate software, hardware, and input devices. The search provides product descriptions, links to vendors, and information on products compatible with Mac OS X. In addition to providing information on assistive technology, this resource is helpful to educators who want to find Mac-compatible special needs instructional software that will provide learning alternatives.

▶ UNIX

Originally developed by Bell Labs in 1971, UNIX has become a popular workstation OS known for its power, flexibility, and portability. There are numerous UNIX OS variations including Linux, BSD, and Solaris (Linux is discussed in greater detail in Chapter 9). Links to information on these systems and others can be found through Yahoo!'s UNIX page <http://dir.yahoo.com/Computers_and_Internet/Software/ Operating_Systems/Unix/>.

Sun Microsystems is building extensive accessibility support into its Solaris operating environment (OE). Solaris is a UNIX-based OE developed by Sun originally to run on Sun's SPARC (**S**calable **P**rocessor **Arch**itecture) workstations. However, Solaris now runs on many other workstations developed by other vendors.

Sun has made an impressive commitment to supporting Open Source accessibility development. Sun received the American Foundation for the Blind (AFB) 2002 Helen Keller Achievement Award for its design of the GNOME desktop accessibility architecture, which provides support for assistive technology compatibility. This Open Source architecture will also benefit users of the Linux OS who use GNOME. Accessibility highlights, features, and future development plans for the GNOME desktop are reviewed online <http://wwws.sun.com/software/star/gnome/accessibility/index.html>. View the online chart, Solaris Accessibility Quick View, to learn about accessibility features and functions of the GNOME 2 Desktop for the Solaris OE <http://wwws.sun.com/software/star/gnome/accessibility/ quickview.html>. GNOME and other Open Source accessibility developments have enormous potential to provide low cost assistive technologies for computer users with disabilities (see Chapter 9). Consult the University of Wisconsin, Madison's Trace Research and Development Center's UNIX and Linux Software Toolkit to learn about available accessibility options <http://trace.wisc.edu/world/computer_ access/unix/unixshar.html>.

▶ Other Resources

The Trace Center's Web site has a comparison chart of OS accessibility features available online. *Operating Systems with built-in Accessibility Features* can be found through the Trace site <http://www.trace.wisc.edu/world/computer_access/compare.html>. More Internet resources related to computers and software are available through the Trace Center's page, *Designing More Usable Computers and Software* <http://trace.wisc.edu/world/computer_access/>. This page provides direct links to the major hardware and software developers' accessibility programs and resources.

The trend toward expanding and improving the built-in accessibility features available on computer operating systems is helping to make computer technology that much more attractive, usable, and valuable to people with disabilities. We are likely to see increasingly sophisticated built-in text-to-speech, speech recognition, and magnification capabilities added in the future. As the computer-using population continues to age, more seniors surfing the Net will certainly be looking for products that come with these advanced utilities.

References

Section 508 Facts: Understanding Section 508 and the Access Board's Standards, The Access Board, Washington, D.C. <http://216.218.205.189/sec508/brochure.htm>.

Section 508 Overview For Consumers: Electronic and Information Technology, Information Technology Technical Assistance and Training Center <http://www.ittatc.org> and <http://www.ittatc.org/technical/consumer_involvement.cfm>.

Section 508 Web site <http://www.section508.gov/>.

Webopedia <http://www.webopedia.com/TERM/U/UNIX.html>.

Chapter 9

The Linux Operating System and Accessible Free Software

By JP Schnapper-Casteras

Introduction to Linux

Linux is an operating system (OS), just like Microsoft Windows or Apple's Mac OS. Linux comes in many shapes and sizes; one popular form is a desktop or workstation deployment. This desktop looks and feels very similar to a traditional graphical desktop environment, complete with windows, icons, mouse, and pointer (WIMP for short). Although Linux is visually similar to popular commercial desktops and OSes, there are some characteristics about Linux that make it very distinct from other OSes.

Free
Linux is free—yes, monetarily free. Although you can go into a computer store and buy a boxed version of Linux, you can also download Linux for free or order a copy for the price of the CD (a couple of dollars), and legally at that. Not only can Linux be freely obtained in a legal manner, much of the software that runs on Linux is released under a license called the GNU General Public License <http://www.gnu.org/copyleft/gpl.html>, which mandates that the

software be freely available. This clearly has drastic implications for the popularity and costs of implementing Linux, as discussed in Chapter 8.

Open Source

The majority of Linux software is also "Open Source," which means that the source code, or programmed instructions that comprise the application, can be freely obtained, modified, and redistributed by anyone. On the other hand, most commercial operating systems and commercial applications are "Closed Source"—only certain designated company employees can view the code and modify the code for authorized personnel to see.

Developed by Volunteers

Since Linux and many Linux applications are Open Source, there are many communities of volunteers and professionals from all over the world who collaborate to update, expand, and improve the software. A developer in one country can modify the source code of his or her word processor to add a feature and then everyone else can benefit from and continue to develop that feature.

Many Shapes, Sizes, and Distributions

There are many shapes, sizes, and flavors or distributions of Linux. The term "Linux" can refer to versions of the operating system that can run on desktops or workstations, Web servers, and high-power clusters of computers (e.g., for scientific computing, rendering graphics). But Linux also comes in smaller, trimmer forms and works on handheld computers, wristwatches, and digital appliances. Linux distributors are vendors that package and copy Linux onto CDs and other media. Distributors often include custom software and configurations along with customer support or printed materials in their boxed set.

Console AND Graphical

One final important property of Linux is that Linux has two different types of applications: console and desktop/graphical. Console applications resemble DOS (Disk Operating System) programs—they are all-text applications that are operated by keyboard, whereas desktop or graphical applications make extensive use of both graphics and the mouse (point and click interface). On the Microsoft Windows or Apple Mac OS platforms, console applications have ceded much of their popularity to graphical counterparts. But on Linux, console applications are still very popular among users and in many cases co-exist with graphical applications. Some Linux users prefer the console interface and many users employ a combination of console and graphical tools to perform daily tasks.

The Linux Landscape

The landscape of Linux consists of many interrelated layers of tools and libraries (collections of functions) that build on top of each other. Using, deploying, or developing for Linux without some understanding of these layers will make it very difficult to understand what and where you are interacting, let alone understand terms and troubleshoot.

Linux's metaphorical terrain has three basic levels: low, mid/high, and application-level (see Figure 9.1). Users interact within the application-level region—navigating their desktop, or utilizing graphical and console tools such as an office suite or a Web browser. In turn, these console and desktop/graphical applications rely on low and mid/high layers of Linux to function. The heart of the low-level layer and the core of Linux is the Linux kernel; the kernel controls the most basic interaction with hardware (e.g., writing to the hard drive, controlling memory usage, sound, drivers). The mid/high-level layer uses the kernel to build libraries of functions and toolkits on which applications are based. The X Windows System <www.xfree86.org> resides in this region and is needed for graphical interfaces, mouse interaction, and the "point and click" interfaces that are so common today. The console environment or "shell" also inhabits this mid/high-level layer; the console environment is required for console or text-based applications. Together these three primary regions of Linux, each with several layers, allow for graphical and console applications and a graphical desktop environment.

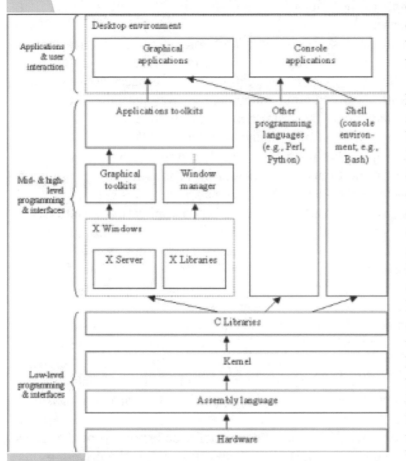

Figure 9.1: Linux Landscape [Reprinted with permission from JP Schnapper-Casteras.]

Linux Accessibility Tools

Console

Three of the most notable console tools are Emacspeak, Speakup, and BRLTTY. Emacspeak <http://emacspeak.sourceforge.net/> is a speech-enabled version of the popular Emacs package <http://www.gnu.org/software/emacs/>, a highly extensible and customizable text-editor. But Emacs is much more than a simple text editor—it provides access to the Internet, to e-mail, news, a calendar, and a variety of other applications. Emacspeak is an "audio desktop" that builds upon Emacs and features Audio User Interfaces (AUIs). Emacspeak's extension of Emacs is a good example of the value of free software and the GNU General Public License.

The audio desktop uses different voices, inflection, and non-speech auditory icons throughout the AUI to provide "rich contextual feedback" <http://emacspeak.sourceforge.net/>. Emacspeak is also ideal for users editing marked up documents (e.g., Web pages with text and tags) or software code; the editor has custom modes for coding and editing in many programming languages via an AUI.

Speakup <http://www.linux-speakup.org/faq.html> is a modification to the Linux kernel that allows for audio access to Linux "from boot-up to shut-down." Speakup speech-enables the console and provides access to virtually all console-based applications. Red Hat® Linux® version 8.0 included Speakup and made it possible to install Linux on any machine without sighted assistance (e.g., via a speech interface). Speakup and Emacspeak take different approaches to speech-enabling applications. Speakup modifies the kernel or core of Linux so that text in the console can be sent to a speech synthesizer, whereas Emacspeak is a standalone application that includes many of its own, richly speech-enabled tools with it. Both console tools have their advantages: Emacspeak has extremely rich AUIs for its included applications, while Speakup provides less rich audio feedback and interaction but provides screen reading abilities to nearly any console application.

Finally, BRLTTY <http://dave.mielke.cc/brltty/> provides access to the Linux console via a Braille display. It contains the drivers for a number of Braille displays, makes it possible to sensibly review or examine the contents of the console screen, and has limited support for speech sythesis. Finally, BRLTTY can fit on a diskette and supports several dozen refreshable Braille displays from a number of manufacturers.

Graphical Desktop

There are two primary desktop environments for Linux: GNOME <http://www.gnome.org/> and KDE <http://www.kde.org/>. Both are extremely mature graphical desktop environments, each with its own suite of applications (e.g., office, Web browser, multimedia tools) and support for multiple languages. Both desktops also have accessibility efforts underway. The GNOME Accessibility Project, backed by Sun Microsystems, Baum Engineering SRL, and others, is the further along of the two, but both accessibility efforts collaborate extensively.

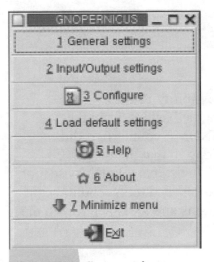

Figure 9.2: **Gnopernicus Main Menu** [Reprinted with permission from Baum Retec AG <http://www.baum.ro/gnopernicus.html>.]

GNOME

The GNOME Accessibility Project <http://developer.gnome.org/projects/gap/> is developing two primary accessibility tools for GNOME: the GNOME Onscreen Keyboard (GOK), and Gnopernicus, an all-in-one screenreader, magnifier, and Braille output tool. As of spring 2003, both tools are still under active development by Sun Microsystems <www.sun.com>, Baum <www.baum.ro>, and the University of Toronto <http://www.utoronto.ca/>.

The main menu of Gnopernicus <http://www.baum.ro/gnopernicus.html>, is included in Figure 9.2.

Note that this menu contains multiple buttons pertaining to settings. Gnopernicus allows for extensive configuration of speech synthesis, Braille rendering, magnification, and keyboard use.

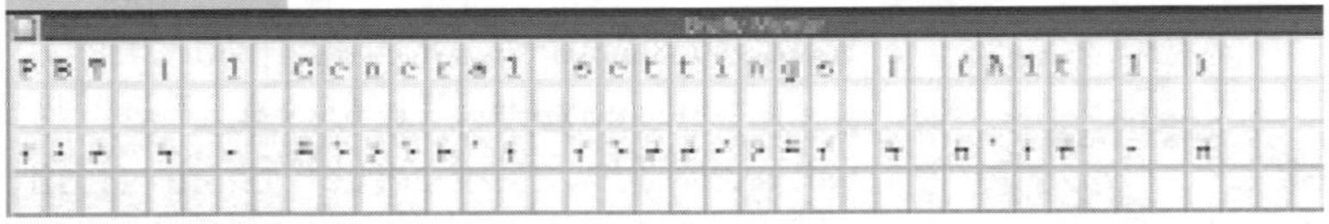

Figure 9.3: **Gnopernicus Braille Monitor** [Reprinted with permission from Baum Retec AG <http://www.baum.ro/gnopernicus.html>.]

The "Braille Monitor," pictured in Figure 9.3, which emulates a Braille access to graphical user interfaces, indicates the presence of push buttons ("PBT") and keyboard shortcuts ("Alt l").

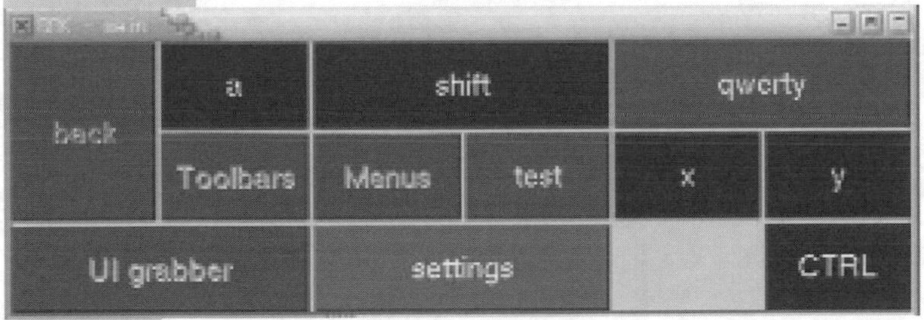

GOK—the GNOME Onscreen Keyboard <http://www.gok.ca/>—is a sophisticated onscreen keyboard and much more. The program also provides access to other graphical UI elements, such as menus and toolbars, and eliminates the need to use keyboard shortcuts.

Figure 9.4: **GNOME Onscreen Keyboard Main Menu** [Reprinted with permission from the University of Toronto Adaptive Technology Resource Centre <http://www.utoronto.ca/atrc/> and <http://www.gok.ca/shots.html>.]

The GNOME Accessibility Project has an advanced accessibility architecture (not surprisingly called the GNOME Accessibility Architecture) that eliminates the need for an "off screen model" or "screen scraping." Instead, the architecture can cleanly examine (i.e., introspect) graphical user interfaces (GUIs) and discover what graphical elements are on the screen as well as their layout, and their properties (e.g., value, role, relationships to other elements). Many people believe that this architecture will make it possible to create graphical user interfaces that are much more accessible, efficient, and natural to use by persons with disabilities.

KDE

At the time of publication, the KDE Accessibility Project <http://accessibility.kde.org> did not have the backing from the corporate and academic realms that its GNOME counterpart did. Accordingly, the project was not as far along in making the KDE desktop accessible, but several useful tools exist, namely KMouseTool, KMag, and KMouth. (Note: KDE applications and tools tend to begin with the letter "K," and GNOME applications and tools begin with the letter "G" or prefix "Gno.")

KMouseTool is a Linux-based KDE program that automatically clicks the mouse after the pointer pauses for a designated amount of time. In addition, in drag mode, the program "virtually" clicks and releases. The main screen is shown in Figure 9.5.

Figure 9.5: KMouseTool Menu [Reprinted with permission from the KDE Accessibility Project <http://accessibility.kde.org>.]

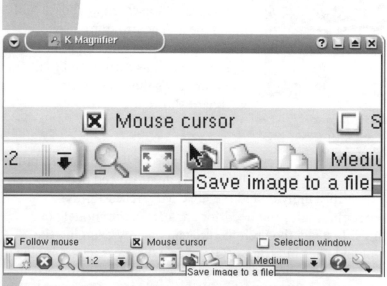

KMag, in Figure 9.6, is an up-and-coming magnifier for the KDE desktop.

Figure 9.6: KMag Window [Reprinted with permission from the KDE Accessibility Project <http://accessibility.kde.org>.]

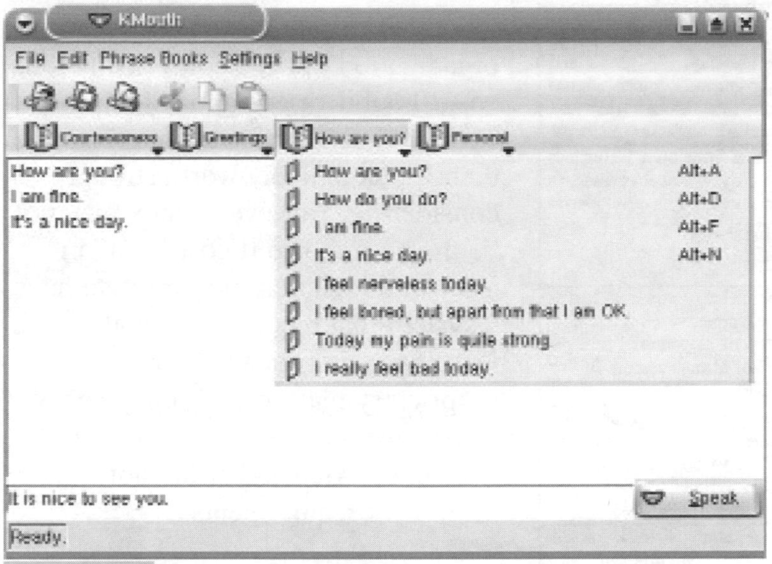

Figure 9.7: KMouth Window [Reprinted with permission from the KDE Accessibility Project <http://accessibility.kde .org>.]

Finally, KMouth (Figure 9.7) is a KDE application that uses a third-party software synthesizer to "speak" for the user via highly configurable phrasebooks and phrases. This application is useful for people who have speech impairments resulting from cerebral palsy, a stroke, or other conditions.

Other Tools

Other particularly noteworthy Linux accessibility tools are Festival, Flite, and Brltty. Festival <http://fife.speech.cs.cmu.edu/festival/> is a high-quality, multi-platform software speech synthesizer developed by the speech group and the Language Technologies Institute at Carnegie Mellon University. A related project is Festvox <http://www.festvox.org/>, a tool for "building" new voices for Festival.

Flite <http://www.speech.cs.cmu.edu/flite/>, which stands for Festival Lite, is a smaller, faster, streamlined version of Festival that can synthesize more quickly and on less powerful devices (e.g., handhelds, old computers). It is interesting to note that engineers at Sun Microsystems recently rewrote Flite in Java™ programming language. This Java™-based synthesizer is called FreeTTS <http://freetts.sourceforge.net/ docs/index.php>, and its existence and availability is surely due to the open source nature of the projects involved.

▶ Deploying Linux

Is Linux Right for You?

The first consideration in deploying Linux at your workplace or home or for a client is "Is Linux right for you?" Figure 9.8 lists common deployment tradeoffs.

Characteristic	Pros	Cons
i. Free	Drastic monetary savings as compared to pay-per-seat or site-licenses with upgrade fees	Any costs are in installation, configuration and deployment, which some argue are harder than on popular proprietary platforms
ii. Open Source	Project developers are often responsive to bug fixing and sometimes to feature requests; you are free to add your own features	Adding your own features is not easy – you may need to find and/or pay a developer to do it for you
iii. Developed by volunteers	A responsive, supportive, and helpful community	Volunteers could leave; development could slow down or stop; initial releases are not always feature-full or stable
iv. Many shapes, sizes, and distributions	Lots of choice; can be deployed on custom small or large platforms (e.g., handhelds or server farms)	The gamut of options also means there is more to learn and a variety of installers, configuration tools, and package formats
v. Console AND graphical	Lots of choice, a high degree of customization, flexibility	There is more to learn, no standard environment or application suite, and some usability problems

Figure 9.8: Deployment Tradeoffs [Reprinted with permission from JP Schnapper-Casteras.]

For example, if your organization's prime concerns include cost, flexibility, customization, choice, or range of available features, then Linux is likely worth strongly considering. However, Linux may not be the best choice if cost is not an issue and it is more important to have a system that requires minimal learning or is similar to popular proprietary platforms. Linux may be a less ideal choice if customization, choice, or extensibility are not prominent requirements.

Learning Linux

For many organizations and technical support teams, Linux is a new, unfamiliar operating system. If this is the case, it is important to allocate enough time to comfortably become familiar with Linux.

First, it is advisable to go to a local bookstore and purchase a book on Linux, ideally with Linux CDs included. Boxed versions of Linux are also available at many electronics stores and often include documentation and a support number (e.g., access to a 1-800 number for 30 days). Secondly, you must decide where you are going to install Linux. It is ideal to install Linux on an extra desktop machine, not your primary workstation. If possible, install Linux on an extra desktop that is not being used or purchase a inexpensive generic machine and use that. If you absolutely must install Linux on your primary workstation, then you will have to "partition" your hard drive so you can run both Linux and your pre-existing Operating System. Be very careful and make sure to carefully read the documentation on partitioning and setting up a dual-boot system. It is possible to accidentally format or erase the contents of the hard drive or to make it difficult to boot your pre-existing OS. When you have perused the book and considered what machine to install Linux on, go ahead and install Linux as specified by the installation guide.

Hands-On Time

After installation, the best way to become familiar with using Linux is simply through hands-on time and experimentation. The necessity of experimentation is another reason why it is ideal to install Linux on a second or an extra desktop machine. Many books about Linux include step-by-step instructions and tutorials about specific parts of, or applications on, Linux. These tutorials can be a very effective way to learn.

Many people find the Linux console is the most difficult component to learn; once again, books and other documentation such as the Linux Documentation Project <http://www.tldp.org/> can greatly ease this transition. Furthermore, the "—help" command suffix is a standard way of entering a help mode or revealing the features of and command line options for console tools.

Finally, chat rooms (e.g., Internet Relay Chat or IRC), mailing lists, and other online discussion forums are invaluable sources for answering questions and troubleshooting. Mailing lists and chat rooms for users often contain the "—users" suffix (e.g., #myapplication-user or <myapplication-user@lists.sourceforge.net>).

Extensions, Customizations, and New Features

One of Linux's main strengths is its enormous customizability and extensibility. As you explore Linux and have hands-on time with the OS, you will likely begin to develop customizations that you or your clients prefer and new features that would be useful. Changes of this sort are particularly necessary for users with disabilities (e.g., low contrast themes, screen reading, customized keyboard shortcuts) or in schools (e.g., where computer systems need to be simpler or to enforce usage policies). Thus it is important to record or write down the customizations you have made so they can be replicated during deployment. In addition, keeping a list of ideal extensions and features is advisable for potential implementation later by technical support staff or members of that particular Open Source project.

Deployment

Hands-on experience, testing, and taking note of the customizations you make are the key pre-deployment steps. When the time comes to actually deploy Linux at your workplace or for your client, consult your technical staff or your local bookstore, library, or online source of documentation. Overall, if you understand the operating system and configuration you are deploying and are careful and considerate in its deployment then your clients' experiences will benefit significantly.

References

On Linux Accessibility:

BRLTTY <http://dave.mielke.cc/brltty/>.

Emacspeak <http://emacspeak.sourceforge.net/>.

Festival <http://fife.speech.cs.cmu.edu/festival/>.

Flite <http://www.speech.cs.cmu.edu/flite/>.

FreeTTS <http://freetts.sourceforge.net/docs/index.php>.

GNOME Accessibility Project
<http://developer.gnome.org/projects/gap/>.

KDE Accessibility Project <http://accessibility.kde.org>.

Linux Accessibility Resource Site (LARS), hosted by the Trace
Research & Development Center at the University of Wisconsin,
Madison <http://trace.wisc.edu/linux/>.

Speakup <http://www.linux-speakup.org/>.

Sphinx <http://fife.speech.cs.cmu.edu/sphinx/> (The CMU Sphinx
Group Open Source Speech Recognition Engines).

On Linux:

DistroWatch <http://www.distrowatch.com/>.

Freshmeat <http://freshmeat.net/>.

GNOME <http://www.gnome.org/>.

KDE <http://www.kde.org/>.

Linux.com <http://www.linux.com/>.

Linux Documentation Project <http://www.tldp.org/>.

The Linux Journal <http://www.linuxjournal.com>.

Linux Online—Distributions and FTP Sites
<http://www.linux.org/dist/>.

Linux.org <http://www.linux.org/>.

Linux Today <http://linuxtoday.com/>.

Linux Weekly News <http://lwn.net/>.

Slashdot <http://slashdot.org/>.

Chapter 10

Mobility Issues and Resources

Many of us take our mobility for granted until we experience some form of restricted movement. A person's movements may be affected as a result of an injury that causes short- or long-term impairment. Mobility challenges can be the result of a congenital condition, a syndrome, a trauma, an illness, or a circumstance that results in debilitation.

Many different syndromes and conditions can have an impact on a person's movement abilities, and there may be considerable variation in the movement characteristics of different people affected by the same condition. Unique factors create unique symptoms. Individuals with differing mobility needs have differing educational and library media center access needs. Therefore, an individual approach must be taken in meeting the needs of people with mobility challenges.

The numbers of students ages six through 21 in the United States with orthopedic impairments served under IDEA rose from 49,340 in 1990–1991 to 71,422 in 1999–2000. This is an increase of 44.8% (**Twenty-third Annual Report to Congress on the Implementation of the Individuals with Disabilities Education Act**, Section II: Student Characteristics <http://www.ed.gov/offices/OSERS/ OSEP/Products/OSEP2001AnlRpt/Section_II.doc>). This category alone does not represent all of the students who could have some type of mobility impairment, as some students listed in other categories such as traumatic brain injury, multiple disabilities, and other health impairments would experience movement challenges.

Online resources provide plenty of information on the many conditions and syndromes that affect movement. The following Web sites may be useful for further investigation on specific conditions that affect movement:

- We Move <http://www.wemove.org/>
- Kids Move <http://www.wemove.org/kidsmove/>
- United Cerebral Palsy <http://www.ucpa.org/>

Wheelchair Accessibility

Facilities

"The average public school was built 42 years ago during the baby boom. About one-third of all public schools are in the oldest condition: built before 1970 and not renovated since 1980" (**Age of School Buildings**, National Center for Education Statistics, Office of Educational Research & Improvement, U.S. Department of Education <http://nces.ed.gov/programs/coe/2000/section4/indicator49.asp>).

The fact that many schools were constructed before inclusive education practices became widespread creates challenges for staff and students with disabilities. Because of the costs associated with renovations, building, room, and floor-to-floor access, issues must be analyzed by district and school staff and addressed according to priority.

Library media specialists should look at the access into the library media center, the library layout, the structures, and resources. Note the areas where possible barriers exist and look for ways that they can be remedied. Some areas and structures may require reorganization or repositioning to provide better access for people with mobility challenges.

"About half of all public schools were enrolled at less than capacity in 1999, but one in five was overcrowded. Schools with 600 or more students were more likely to be severely overcrowded than smaller schools" (**Overcrowding in Schools**, National Center for Education Statistics, Office of Educational Research & Improvement, U.S. Department of Education <http://nces.ed.gov/programs/coe/2001/section4/indicator45.asp>).

Library media center access can become more difficult for students with mobility challenges if the school is overcrowded. How easily can students using wheelchairs, crutches, and other mobility aids travel through crowded corridors and seating areas? If the facilities do not provide adequate space for the numbers of students being served, then students with mobility issues may find the lack of room to maneuver presents an access barrier.

The University of Washington's DO-IT Program provides online resources to assist with facility accessibility review and evaluation:

- Equal Access: Computer Labs <http://www.washington.edu/doit/Brochures/Technology/comp.access.html>
- Universal Access: Making Library Resources Accessible to People with Disabilities <http://www.washington.edu/doit/UA/PRESENT/libres.html>
- General Library Access Overheads <http://www.washington.edu/doit/UA/PRESENT/ohlib.pdf>

Furniture

The furniture and related structures within the library media center include shelving, stacks, publication stands, desks, tables, carrels, check-out desks, general seating, computer workstations, file cabinets, and miscellaneous items such as book carts. One style of seating, table, or publication display system may be fine for the majority of library users, but many libraries are diversifying their furnishings, material displays, and storage structures to meet the needs of users with disabilities. Modular furniture is popular in many libraries, as it lends itself to reconfiguration and provides flexibility for the reallocation and usability of space.

There are ergonomic considerations that we should be aware of when it comes to repetitive and prolonged computer use. *An Introduction to Ergonomics and Workstation Design* (Thomas, M., 2001) is available online <http://www.techconsult.org/ERGONOMICS/ERGONOMICSWP.HTML>. This paper provides a very good overview of statistics, on-the-job injuries, considerations for office and workstation design, preventative maintenance, and a glossary of ergonomic terms.

A "one size fits all" layout and furnishing plan provides fewer options for comfort and access to people who cannot work at a standard-height or standard-width table or desk. If the user in a wheelchair is unable to get close enough to the computer workstation to use the computer, it creates a barrier to information access. It may be possible to modify a standard computer workstation to accommodate a wheelchair by simply raising the height of the desk by placing blocks under the legs.

However, some people may need more advanced modifications or greater flexibility in order to access the technology properly. There is an online document available through the Texas Technology Access Project called *Designing an Accessible Workstation* <http://tatp.edb.utexas.edu/library/wkstn.html>. There are different styles of accessible computer workstations available through a range of vendors. Some of these products offer motorized or hand-crank height adjustment so that they can be quickly set up for multiple access requirements. Online resellers, such as EnableMart.com <http://www.enablemart.com>, provide accessible workstations and other assistive technology products.

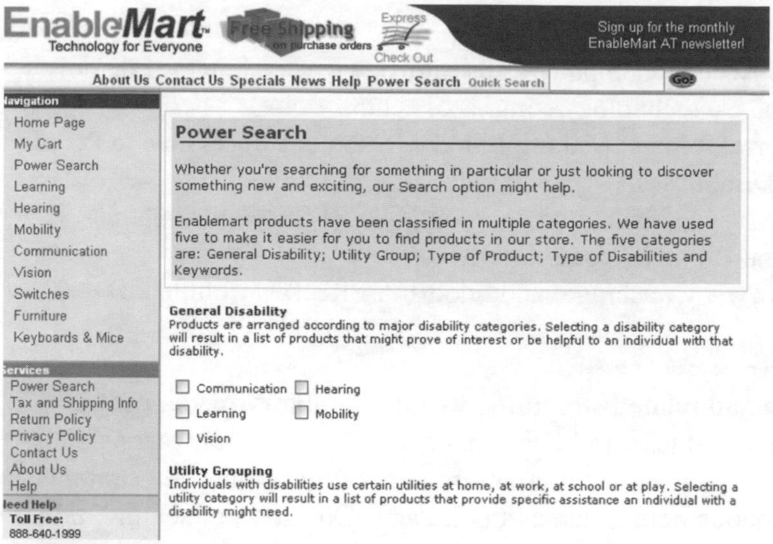

Figure 10.1: EnableMart.com [Reprinted with permission from EnableMart.com <http://www.enablemart.com>.]

Special Services

Special services are often provided to postsecondary and public library patrons who have disabilities. Some examples of enhanced services include: catalog assistance, book/journal retrieval, photocopying, browsing assistance, and wayfinding/accompanying. More libraries are now providing instruction on the use of adaptive technology for their users who have disabilities.

In the K–12 school setting, some students who have disabilities will have the assistance of a full-time or part-time support worker. Student assistants can also help with general assistance activities such as book retrieval, photocopying, and browsing.

Alternative Computer Access Technologies

A standard mouse works just fine for most of us, although some students may need to gain skills to operate a mouse effectively. Practice may help for students who find it difficult to control the computer with a mouse. Online *Mouse Skills* are available and could help some students learn to use a mouse <http://www.customsolutions.us/mouse/>.

Other students may need other options in order to successfully input and access information.

Touch Screens

When a touch screen is added to a computer monitor, it enables finger-to-screen control of the software. Users can make selections, move objects, and pull down menus without using a keyboard. Some monitors are available with built-in touch screens. Although this is convenient, if the monitor breaks down, the touch screen cannot be installed on another monitor. Add-on touch screens can be purchased through different vendors and resellers. It is important to order the size that will properly fit the monitor. Although add-on touch screens may be accidentally knocked off the screen, they can be moved to a different monitor, of compatible size, when necessary.

Mouse Alternatives

In addition to the wide variety of optical, trackball, joystick, and wheel mouse alternatives, there are other hardware options for people who have mobility problems. Specialized foot, cheek, or other bodily-activated switch technologies provide hands-free computer access for users who can interact with the computer using another area of the body. Appropriately mounted single- or multiple-switch systems can be used to access software programs. Switches come in a wide variety of styles and activation categories to meet the individual needs of people with different motor characteristics. Some of these options require the installation of companion hardware such as a switch interface. A freeware program, *SAW4*, which allows Windows to be accessed by one or two switches, or a joystick, trackball, or head pointer, is available through the Oxford ACE Centre <http://www.ace-centre.org.uk/html/software/saw/sawalt1.html>.

Alternative Keyboards and Hands-Free Text-Entry Software

There are numerous specialized keyboard options available. These include color-coded, large print, adjustable, one-handed, and ergonomically designed keyboards. Also available are specialized keyboards that can be used with customized overlays.

Onscreen keyboards create a virtual interface for computer users who have difficulty with a real keyboard. Recent versions of the Microsoft Windows operating system come with a built-in onscreen keyboard. Users can find this utility by clicking on *start/programs/accessories/accessibility*. Some people use the onscreen keyboard with a touch-screen, a head-pointing, or an eye-tracking device to enter data. More advanced onscreen keyboard software can also be purchased for Windows and Macintosh operating systems.

Speech-recognition software is a dictation text-entry option. Speech-recognition software is not an appropriate technology for all students. There are considerable training demands, and environmental and user characteristics, that influence productivity outcomes. Library media specialists will generally not have the time to individually train students to use this technology. However, students who have received training and are able to use the software on a laptop computer could use it in a library seminar room to avoid disrupting other students. ScanSoft's *Dragon NaturallySpeaking* and IBM's *ViaVoice* are two of the popular commercial products available. Web resources providing information about speech recognition include:

- Computing Out Loud <http://www.out-loud.com/>
- Key Steps to High Speech Recognition Accuracy <http://www.emicrophones.com/articles/Keys_to_dictation.asp>

■ The Dragon NaturallySpeaking Guide
<http://lib1.store.vip.sc5.yahoo.com/lib/sayican/onlineBook.html>

Head-Pointer, Eye-Tracking, and Speech-Navigation Technologies

Head-pointer, eye-tracking, and speech-navigation technologies can replace the use of a mouse, trackball, or joystick for people who cannot use their hands. Head-pointer and eye-tracking systems rely on a wireless optical sensor that can be mounted on a desktop or laptop computer. The sensor tracks a tiny disposable target (dot) that can be placed on the user's forehead or eyeglasses. The user's head movements will enable the movement of the computer mouse pointer. Selection can be accomplished with switch or dwell activations. These technologies may require specific combinations of hardware and software. One hands-free computer control system, *CameraMouse* <http://www.cameramouse.com>, uses a standard USB camera to control a computer using head or finger movements. This product is expensive, but a free trial is available. *VisualMouse* can be downloaded for free from MouseVision, Inc., <http://www.mousevision.com/ assistivetech.html>. The company intends to give *VisualMouse* to people with disabilities for free without a time limit. *Dasher* <http://www.inference.phy.cam.ac.uk/dasher/> is another innovative free text-entry system. A speech-navigation system that provides complete hands-free voice computer control is Commodio's *Qpointer Voice* software <http://www.commodio.com/>.

▶ Other Support and Access Devices

Other devices, in addition to computer technologies, may provide greater independence for students with mobility challenges.

Page Turners

Mechanized page turners, such as the *GEWA Page Turner BLV-6* available through ZYGO Industries, Inc., <http://www.zygo-usa.com> in Portland, Oregon, are expensive products. However, these devices provide greater reading independence for people who are unable to turn pages backward and forward by themselves.

Book Stands

For students who have difficulty supporting books by themselves, a reading stand or book holder provides flexibility. Office supply stores carry simple book and document holders. The Levo Bookholder <http://www.bookholder.com> is a more adaptable product that can be adjusted for someone reading in standing, sitting, or lying positions.

References

Age of School Buildings, National Center for Education Statistics, Office of Educational Research & Improvement, U.S. Department of Education <http://nces.ed.gov/programs/coe/2000/section4/indicator49.asp>.

Designing an Accessible Workstation, Texas Technology Access Project <http://tatp.edb.utexas.edu/library/wkstn.html>.

Overcrowding in Schools, National Center for Education Statistics, Office of Educational Research & Improvement, U.S. Department of Education <http://nces.ed.gov/programs/coe/2001/section4/indicator45.asp>.

Thomas, M., *An Introduction to Ergonomics and Workstation Design*, 2001 <http://www.techconsult.org/ERGONOMICS/ERGONOMICSWP.HTML>.

Twenty-third Annual Report to Congress on the Implementation of the Individuals with Disabilities Education Act, Section II: Student Characteristics <http://www.ed.gov/offices/OSERS/OSEP/Products/OSEP2001AnlRpt/Section_II.doc>.

Chapter 11

Print Disability Issues and Resources

Obviously, a collection of print resources alone just won't work for students with wide-ranging visual impairments and print disabilities. The revolutionary proliferation of blind and low vision technologies is one of the most impressive fields of assistive technology development today. These products are helping people with visual impairments to work, play, and enjoy daily living with greater independence.

Hardware

Assorted computer-related and standalone devices provide information access options for blind and low vision students in a library media center.

Closed Circuit Television (CCTV)

The CCTV, also known as a video magnifier, is a standalone device that can magnify small objects or print. It looks like a TV or computer monitor on a specialized stand, and it allows a book, other print material, or objects such as pill bottles and craft materials to be used or examined through the magnified image on the screen. Students with low vision can use a CCTV in the library media center or another location, allowing more independent access to reading materials. A CCTV allows a student to review materials according to his or her schedule, without having to request that someone photocopy and enlarge the print of the pages that he or she wants to read. A CCTV that is secured on a wheeled trolley will allow a student to move the device to different areas. Smaller portable CCTVs are also available.

Scanners and Headphones

Scanners equipped with optical character recognition software (OCR) allow students and staff to convert print resources to digital text. For example, a textbook chapter can be scanned page by page on a flatbed scanner connected to a computer. The OCR software processes the print from the pages, converting it to electronic text in a word processing document or another application. Once the text is available on the word processor, it can be enlarged or manipulated in other ways so that it is more readable. The text can also be read by a synthesized voice if the computer has text-to-speech software installed. This type of software is very helpful for students with reading and visual disabilities. Head-phones will allow the user to listen to the textbook chapter without disrupting other library users. If students prefer to use ear buds or another type of headset, they can be encouraged to bring their own earphones to the library media center.

Other types of scanners, including single-page scanners and handheld scanners with OCR, are also available. However, the flatbed scanner is the best of these options for scanning bound books. Specialized scanning reading machines have been developed, such as BAUM's Poet Compact <http://www.baum.de/English/poet-comp.htm>. This standalone reading machine will automatically convert scanned print materials to speech output.

Large Monitors and Magnifying Monitor Screens

Many libraries are now installing larger computer screens on their computers to help their patrons view Internet and other electronic content. Popular screen sizes are 15, 17, 19, and 21 inches. The resolution should be adjusted for optimal image quality when upgrading to a larger screen. The screen resolution refers to the number of dots (pixels) that can be displayed on the screen. An online article, *Screen Size & Resolution* <http://www.naplestech.com/pages/resolution.htm>, explains more about this topic.

Add-on computer magnification screens, such as the iMAG GlareFilter <http://www.glareshield.com/imag.html> and the CompuMag <http://www.monitor-magnifier.com/>, can be installed on the computer's screen.

Customized Keyboards

As mentioned in the previous chapter on technology for mobility-related disabilities, there are large print keyboards available, such as BigKeys. Color-coded keys can also be added to improve contrast <http://www.keytops.com/keytops/color-keyboards.htm>. To avoid the expense of purchasing a brand new keyboard, it is possible to customize a regular keyboard by adding stick-on large print, high-contrast, or tactile letters and numbers, or Braille key labels. These can be ordered from different distributors, but you can look at some examples of these through the Dynamic Living Web site <http://dynamic-living.com/keyboard_labels_big_print.htm>. Similar sticker products are sometimes available for free through low vision software companies at conferences and trade shows.

Braille Display and Braille Output

Braille display technologies, Braille printers, and related devices are expanding the potential of computer use for independent learning and the career advancement of students with visual disabilities. Much of this technology is very expensive for an individual or a family to acquire. The support of educational institutions and agencies in supplying enabling technology is essential for blind students who must depend on tactile and auditory feedback to gain access to electronic information.

Refreshable Braille displays are devices that allow blind students to read the computer screen content with their fingertips. This display device moves a series of pins up and down as it translates the text on the computer's screen into Braille dots that are formed by the pin movements. The user receives a line-by-line translation of the text into refreshable Braille.

Consult the American Foundation for the Blind's Web site to learn about the range of Braille technologies and the manufacturers' contact information <http://www.afb.org/info_document_view.asp?documentid=1282>.

Software

Literacy and blind and low vision support software is readily available from developers and resellers around the world. These products range in level of sophistication. The more expensive products generally have enhanced configuration options and specialized features. However, there are some freeware products available that can be downloaded without expense for use by students and staff in school and at home. A few resources are listed below:

- **_ReadPlease 2003_** <http://www.readplease.com/> is a text-to-speech software product for Windows.
- **_HELP Read_** <http://www.pixi.com/~reader1/index/index.html> is text-to-speech software. Download instructions and tutorials are available online.
- **_Apple Macintosh Software Toolkit_** <http://www.trace.wisc.edu/world/computer_access/mac/macshare.html> is an online resource

developed by the Trace Center at the University of Wisconsin. A selection of accessibility enhancing software downloads is available through this link.

- ■ **The Screen Magnifiers Homepage** <http://www.magnifiers.org/cgi-bin/links/search.cgi?query= freeware/ gives information about freeware and shareware magnification software.

Blind and Low Vision

Screen magnification and Braille translation software provide visually impaired computer users with the tools they need to independently surf the Web and access electronic information.

Braille translation software, available through Duxbury Systems <http://www.duxburysystems.com/> and BrailleMaster <http://www.braillemaster.com/>, allows a user to translate text to a Braille printer or a Braille file. It can be used to facilitate tactile access to text-based resources for students who are blind.

Screen magnification software allows the user to expand the size of computer screen images or print. Simple screen magnifiers can be used to incrementally expand the screen contents from 2X to 16X (or more) the normal view size. Advanced screen magnifiers are available that include text-to-speech capabilities, built-in OCR, and assorted viewing options. A person using an advanced screen magnification product can select a Web page, expand the text size, alter the text and background color combinations, and listen to selections read by one of a variety of customizable synthesized male or female voices. Word tracking features allow the viewer to follow each highlighted word as it is read. Advanced screen magnification software products provide visual and auditory support for individuals with visual impairments.

Learn More about Advanced Magnification and Screen Reading Software

ZoomText 8.0 from Ai Squared

ZoomText 8.0 is available in two product versions:

- ZoomText Magnifier—a standalone screen magnifier
- ZoomText Magnifier/Screen Reader—an integrated magnifier and screen reader

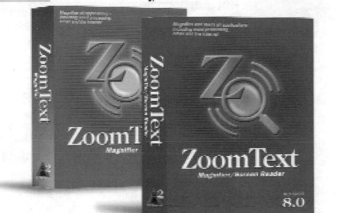

Figure 11.1: ZoomText 8.0 Magnifier and Magnifier/ Screen Reader [Product information, box and screen shots reprinted with permission from Ai Squared <http:// www.aisquared.com>.]

System Requirements

- Pentium II or higher
- Windows XP, Windows Millennium, Windows 2000, or Windows 98
- High Color (16 bit) or True Color (24 or 32 bit) display driver
- Minimum 128 MB RAM (256 MB recommended)
- Sound card

Ai2 Contact Information

P.O. Box 669
Manchester Center, VT 05255 USA
(802) 362-3612
<sales@aisquared.com>
<www.aisquared.com>

The *Screen Magnifiers Homepage* <http://www.magnifiers.org> provides information on many of the top screen magnification companies and products. User satisfaction surveys are conducted every year, and there's a download page <http://www.magnifiers.org/links/ Download_Software/Screen_Magnifiers/> to help users find trial products for the Windows, Mac, and UNIX/Linux operating systems.

Literacy

Software for literacy support includes screen-reader utilities and more advanced products that help students with reading and composition activities. Again, the most expensive products in this category offer a collection of useful features that can be used alone or in combination to assist with the reading and writing process. The *LD OnLine Tech Guide* provides a listing of commercial software and other products that may help:

- Reading Resources
  <http://www.ldonline.org/ld_indepth/technology/product_list/reading.html>
- Writing Resources
  <http://www.ldonline.org/ld_indepth/technology/product_list/writing.html>

Screen-reader software allows a computer user with reading challenges to listen to a text file, either an online file, or a scanned document, read by a synthesized voice. Most products allow users to adjust the voice quality to suit their personal listening needs.

Word-prediction software provides assistance to students who have difficulty with spelling. It generates a changing list of word choices that correspond to the letters being entered on a word processing document such as *MS Word*. This can help students who know the first couple of letters of a word, but aren't sure how to spell the rest of the word. When the user spots the word he or she needs, he or she can quickly select it and it will instantly appear on the document. This software can also help slow typists and people with mobility challenges, as it reduces the number of keystrokes needed to compose a document. Word-prediction products developed by different software companies range in their level of sophistication. Simple word-prediction products may only offer several words as selection options. The more expensive products offer more word choices, multiple word prediction, and features such as the speaking of listed words by a synthesized voice.

Figure 11.2: Student using Kurzweil reading technology. [Reprinted with permission from Kurzweil Educational Systems <http://www.kurzweiledu.com>.]

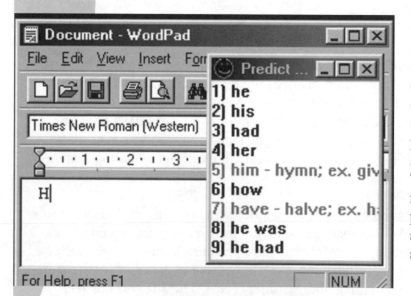

Figure 11.3: Aurora Prediction window adjusts the word choices whenever a new letter is typed. [Reprinted with permission from Aurora Systems, Inc., <http://www.aurora-systems.com>.]

Tactile Resources

Tactile materials and maps can assist blind students to grasp concepts in math, geography, and other areas. Some companies provide custom tactile mapping services for buildings such as schools and libraries. These maps can assist blind patrons with orientation and navigation in unfamiliar facilities.

- Tactile Vision, Inc. <http://www.tactilevisioninc.com/>
- Creative Adaptations for Learning <http://www.cal-s.org/>
- American Printing House for the Blind <http://www.aph.org>

Descriptive Video Service

Descriptive video service (DVS) is provided through the Media Access Group at WGBH (read about the Media Access Group captioning services in Chapter 12). DVS videos include additional narration of characters' gestures, settings, costume descriptions, and other details of a presentation that are not accessible to people with visual impairments. Professionally written and read, DVS scripts of additional details accompany video productions and help to engage people with visual impairments so that they can follow and enjoy the plot, performance, or event. DVS video titles currently available through the DVS Home Video catalog can be viewed online <http://main.wgbh.org/wgbh/pages/mag/resources/dvs-home-video-catalogue.html>. An online guide explaining how to record DVS on a VCR is also available <http://main.wgbh.org/wgbh/pages/mag/resources/guides/mag_guide_vol1.html>.

Web Accessibility

With such an incredible amount of electronic information available to students on the Internet, the Web has enormous potential to open new doors to learning and career opportunities for students with disabilities. There are a growing number of online university, vocational, and high-school courses that are Web accessible. These opportunities provide greater learning flexibility for students with mobility impairments and other disabilities.

However, the issue of how information is presented on the Internet and how easily users can access it determines how usable Web content will be for a wide range of learning requirements. Learning about accessible Web site design concepts, browser accessibility enhancements, and add-on assistive technology options are important steps toward helping students with disabilities exploit the potential of the Internet to reach their goals.

Browser Accessibility Options

A Web browser is a software application that can locate and display Web pages. Graphical browsers can display text and graphics. Most modern browsers can also display multimedia information including sound and video. There are more Web browser options available than the browsers that will be discussed in this chapter. To learn about other browsers, visit the online resources listed:

- Webmonkey Browser Chart
  <http://hotwired.lycos.com/webmonkey/reference/browser_chart/>
- Stroud's CWSApps <http://cws.internet.com/web.html>
- Browsers with Built-in Voice or Other Access Features
  <http://trace.wisc.edu/world/web/#bbvo>

Internet Explorer, developed by Microsoft Corporation, is distributed for free and can be downloaded from the Internet Explorer homepage <http://www.microsoft.com/windows/ie/default.asp>. Step-by-step tutorials on Internet Explorer (versions 5 and 6) accessibility options are available <http://www.microsoft.com/enable/training/default.aspx>. These tutorials can be reproduced for educational purposes.

Netscape Navigator is a popular browser developed by Netscape Communications Corporation located in Mountain View, California. Navigator can run on all major platforms (Windows, Macintosh, UNIX/Linux). Information about the latest version's (Netscape Navigator 7.0) features can be reviewed online <http://channels.netscape.com/ns/browsers/browsing.jsp>. Text size can be easily adjusted through the *View* heading on the Navigator toolbar. Changes can be made to the text and background color combinations as well as fonts by selecting *Edit/Preferences* on the toolbar.

Mozilla is an Open Source Web browser (read about Open Source in Chapter 9). Mozilla.org was launched when Netscape announced in 1998 that they would release the Netscape browser source code. Up-to-date information about Mozilla accessibility development is available online <http://www.mozilla.org/projects/ui/accessibility/>.

Opera Browser, developed by Oslo-based Opera Software ASA, is compatible with multiple operating systems and is available for download free from the company's Web site <http://www.opera.com>. Opera has some outstanding accessibility features built into the system to support users with vision and mobility impairments. The mouse gestures available in Opera can boost productivity for all users <http://www.opera.com/features/mouse/>. Review information about all the features on its accessibility page <http://www.opera.com/features/access/index.dml>.

JustVanilla is a Web-based subscription software service that provides customizable accessibility features to help make the Internet more usable for people with disabilities. A companion talking browser, *VanillaTalk*, can also be purchased. More information is available online at <http://www.justvanilla.com>.

Web Site Design Standards

The way that a Web site is designed can influence how accessible the information is for computer users with disabilities. Those who are blind, or those who have color blindness, low vision, or seizure disorders, can run into problems using some Web sites. Web sites that are designed with a lot of multimedia features, flashing graphics, images without descriptions, and poorly contrasting text and background colors can make it difficult or impossible for some visitors with disabilities to access the information. Accessible Web site design is especially important when selecting appropriate educational sites for students with disabilities. Consideration of accessible Web site design principles and standards is also important for educational institutions that want to provide online learning opportunities and make their district and school sites accessible for the widest possible audience.

W3C Consortium

The World Wide Web Consortium (W3C) <http://www.w3.org/> is an organization that works to develop Web standards with the goal of leading the World Wide Web to its full potential. The W3C has a very strong commitment to universal access. Founded in 1994, the W3C now has over 450 members and approximately 70 full-time staff members. A seven-point summary of W3C's goals can be found through its site <http://www.w3.org/Consortium/Points/>.

W3C Web Accessibility Initiative

 The W3C's work in the area of Web accessibility for people with disabilities is carried out through its Web Accessibility Initiative (WAI) <http://www.w3.org/WAI/>. An overview of the WAI is presented in an online slide presentation <http://www.w3.org/Talks/WAI-Intro/slide1-0.html>. The slide maker software that created this presentation allows users to view the slides in different accessible styles. The W3C Slidemaker Tool software can be freely downloaded <http://www.w3.org/Talks/slidemaker/YYMMsub/>. The key concepts of accessible Web design are listed on the WAI quick tips page <http://www.w3.org/WAI/References/QuickTips/>.

Trace Center's Designing More Usable Web Sites

The Trace Research and Development Center at the University of Wisconsin, Madison, has a well-organized and comprehensive page of links on its site related to accessible Web site design <http://trace.wisc.edu/world/web/>. This is an excellent resource that lists information about guidelines, organizations, projects, and useful tools for Internet users and Webmasters. Some tools listed on the site help to identify Web site accessibility issues. These tools can help educators assess whether a site complies with accessibility standards.

Testing Tools

A Web site may have an accessibility logo displayed on the index or homepage to identify it as a standards-compliant accessible Web site. Explanation of the *W3C* and *Bobby* icons can be found through the following links:

- Bobby logos <http://bobby.watchfire.com/bobby/html/en/icon.jsp>
- W3C logos <http://www.w3.org/WAI/WCAG1-Conformance.html>
- W3C Authoring Tool Accessibility Guidelines (ATAG) conformance logos <http://www.w3.org/WAI/ATAG10-Conformance.html>

Sites with W3C or Bobby logos comply with certain standards or have been tested to determine whether the site is designed according to standards. Links to a sample of online testing tools are listed below:

- W3C HTML Validator <http://validator.w3.org/>
- W3C CSS Validator <http://jigsaw.w3.org/css-validator/>
- Bobby WorldWide <http://bobby.watchfire.com/bobby/html/en/index.jsp)
- Lynx Viewer <http://www.delorie.com/web/lynxview.html>

Other Web site repair and evaluation tools are listed through the W3C Web Accessibility Initiative <http://www.w3.org/WAI/ER/existingtools.html>.

The Information Technology Technical Assistance and Training Center (ITTATC) provides a free online course that teaches techniques for creating accessible Web sites. People who would like to learn the basics about designing an accessible Web site can register online for the ITTATC Web Accessibility course <http://www.ittatc.org/training/webcourse/>. The WebAIM site <http://www.webaim.org> also provides online training services related to Web site accessibility awareness and design.

▶ References

Darby, Sue, *Enhancing the Accessibility of Digital Television for Visually Impaired People*, RNIB, May 29, 1997 <http://www.rnib.org.uk/wesupply/products/digtv.htm#23>.

Hamcrly, J., et al, ***Freeing the Source: The Story of Mozilla***, O'Reilly
    Online Catalog, January 1999
    <http://www.oreilly.com/catalog/opensources/book/netrev.html>.
Introduction to Adaptive Computer Technology, Lighthouse International
    <http://www.lighthouse.org/resources_adaptive_tech.htm>.
Pash, Anthony, ***Designing for Access to the Web for Blind and Visually
    Impaired Users***, National Library of Canada, February 25, 1998
    <http://www.nlc-bnc.ca/9/1/p1-251-e.html>.

Chapter 12

Hearing Impairments

Library media specialists need to have information about the students in their school with hearing impairments. These students will need to use the library media center on an individual basis, but they will also be using the services as part of a class for group instruction such as orientation sessions, book talks, and librarian-led lessons. Students with hearing impairments will display wide variation in the communication methods that they use, and their abilities to socialize with others and to understand spoken communication through lip reading or signing.

Some students may have normal hearing but have difficulty grasping auditory information as the result of a central auditory processing disorder (CAPD). This condition may be undiagnosed in some children who have not had a thorough assessment by an audiologist. Students with CAPD may have difficulty filtering the relevant instruction or auditory information when there are distracting sounds or levels of noise in the room. CAPD can be a source of frustration for students, parents, and educators in the school and home environments. Read more about this condition at the following links:

- Central Auditory Processing Disorder, Konde, S. <http://www.kidshealth.org/parent/medical/ears/central_auditory.html>
- Central Auditory Processing Disorders (CAPD's), Paton, J. <http://www.ldonline.org/ld_indepth/process_deficit/capd_paton.html>

Instructional Strategies

Whether instruction will be given to students in the library media center or another setting, students with hearing impairments and CAPD need to be given special consideration. This may be difficult if there are several classes of students using the library media center at one time, resulting in a heightened noise level. Where possible, try to provide instruction to students in a quiet area or in a seminar room. Encourage students with CAPD or hearing impairments to sit away from sources of noise and distraction.

Library media specialists and teachers can further assist these students by providing visual information in the form of notes, instructions, and outlines written on handouts, a blackboard, a white board, or an overhead projector. When speaking to students who rely on lip reading, position yourself within view of the students (approximately four feet away), with the light source behind the students rather than the speaker. Avoid obstructing the student's ability to lip read by having anything in or in front of your mouth while speaking and giving instructions. Speak in complete sentences and try to have visual examples to help students understand what is being said. If the student is using an interpreter, the interpreter should be close to the student. Realize that the student will require some processing time to interpret the signs and ask questions. The library media specialist or teacher should look at the student when giving instruction, not the interpreter. Try to face the student as much as possible during instruction and communication. Speak sentences a bit more slowly and encourage students to tape record lectures.

When the instructor or students are reading from a book, arrange for the student with a hearing impairment to sit next to someone who can point to the section in the book that is being read and provide cues when discussion or questions are taking place. This type of assistance can reduce confusion when activities change during the lesson. It is very helpful to the student if the library media specialist or teacher repeats the questions asked by class members before answering them. The student with a hearing impairment sitting at the front of the room or near the instructor will often miss communication that is coming from people sitting behind, beside, or in front of him or her.

When presenting multimedia materials to students, think about the needs of students with hearing impairments. If you are showing slides, videos, or films that have a script available, make a copy of it for the students who will need it. Present captioned media when available. If the student works with an interpreter, try to provide information to the interpreter in advance so that the script or presentation format can be reviewed. For example, if the lights will be turned off for a presentation, the interpreter will want to arrange a light source so that signing will be visible to students with hearing impairments. Avoid using audio resources, such as tapes, CDs, and records, to present information in class. It is also important to inform a substitute library media specialist or instructor that there is a student with a hearing impairment in the class or program.

Assistive Listening Devices

An assistive listening device (ALD) may be helpful to some students with CAPD or hearing impairments. The design of an ALD is different from a hearing aid in that the microphone of the ALD is separate from the rest of the device so that it can be located at the source of the sound, which is being targeted for amplification. In contrast, the microphone of a hearing aid is built into the device that is attached to the wearer's ear. This design acts to amplify all sounds and makes the hearing aid more functional in a wide variety of settings. Because the ALD is set up to amplify a specific sound source, such as a telephone, television, or speaker's voice, its applications are limited to specific listening situations, which may include the library media center or classroom. An ALD may be an appropriate form of AT to help a variety of students with attention deficit disorders or listening difficulties, and can complement the use of a hearing aid.

There are different types of assistive listening devices. Although these devices use different types of technology, they all work to pick up the sound from the targeted source and deliver it to the receiver by way of speakers, headphones, ear buds, or a neck loop. Some hearing aids can also receive ALD transmissions without the use of an additional receiver. Commonly used ALDs include FM systems, induction loops, and infrared systems.

Some students with hearing impairments, CAPD, and attention deficits use a personal FM system to help them hear instruction better in a complex learning environment. The student has a small receiver with a volume control that is attached to earphones or ear buds. The teacher clips on the transmitting microphone while instructing the class. The student with the FM receiver and headset is the only one in the class who will pick up the amplified sound. The student is able to take this portable device to different classes in the school. However, the success of this strategy depends on the willingness of the student and instructors to integrate the technology in a consistent, subtle, and non-stigmatizing way. Some students may resist using a personal FM system if they feel it draws unwanted attention to them.

More classrooms are starting to install sound field systems. These are FM wireless microphone public address (PA) systems that amplify the teacher's voice through system speakers set up around the room. The advantages of a sound field system are that all students in the class benefit from the amplified instruction, receivers are not necessary, instructor voice strain is reduced, and the system may be less stigmatizing than implementing a personal system for an individual student.

Induction loop technology is used for some facilities, such as theatres, as a fixed method of providing access for the hearing impaired. The system has an amplifier and a wire (loop) that is installed along the perimeter of the room. These systems use electromagnetic waves for transmission. Wireless reception of the sound is enabled when the amplifier is hooked up to the sound source or public address system. This system allows people who use a hearing aid with a Telecoil (T-Coil/T-Switch) to pick up the amplified sound without the use of another receiver. Other audience members must use a receiver.

Infrared (IR) systems are used in courtrooms, theatres, and convention centers. Sound is transmitted via light waves to receivers worn by users. Interference caused by sunlight means that this system is not suitable for outdoor use.

Some companies that provide assistive listening devices are:

- Phonic Ear <http://www.phonicear.com/>
- Telex Communications <http://www.telex.com/>
- Hearit Company <http://www.hearitllc.com/>
- Audio Enhancement <http://www.audioenhancement.com/>
- Custom AllHear Systems, Inc. <http://www.customallhear.com/>; this company also distributes a "traffic light" noise level management device that some schools are using

Western Oregon University has developed a Web page with some good resources on educational issues related to hearing impairments. The online presentation *Demystifying Assistive Listening Devices*, by Cheryl D. Davis, Ph.D., is available here in slide and text-only formats <http://www.wou.edu/education/sped/nwoc/info.htm>.

Captioning

Library media specialists should be aware of captioning technologies and services that enhance learning resources for students with hearing impairments. Captioning converts the audio component of a video, a film, or software into text that can be read on the screen or monitor. Background noises, music, and other sounds are described as text along with the program narration or character dialogue. In this way, captions differ from subtitles used in foreign films. Subtitles are presented for a hearing audience and do not include audio information, other than the translated dialogue or narration. Captions are classified as closed or open. Closed captions can be hidden on the viewing screen unless they are made visible using a decoder. Closed captions usually appear as white letters in a black box. Open captions are always visible on the viewing screen and do not require a decoder. Open captions usually appear as white letters outlined in black. Captions help people who have hearing impairments to more fully understand a program.

The Captioned Media Program (CMP) <http://www.cfv.org/>, which is funded through the U.S. Department of Education, has over 4,000 open-captioned videos, CD-ROMs, and DVDs available in its free loan program. This collection is available to individuals who are deaf or hard of hearing, and their parents and teachers. The registration form, which is only available for individuals, educational programs, and organizations in the United States and its territories, is available online <http://www.cfv.org/register.asp>. Information about captioning for educators and parents can be found through the CMP site <http://www.cfv.org/caaibrowse.asp> along with links to available captioned resources:

- Captioned Media Program Catalog
  <http://www.cfv.org/cmpcatalog.asp>
- Captioned media from other sources
  <http://www.cfv.org/capmediaother.asp>

Captioning equipment vendors and a glossary of captioning terminology are listed in an online document available through the CMP <http://www.cfv.org/caai/nadh23.pdf>

The Media Access Group at Boston public broadcaster WGBH <http://main.wgbh.org/wgbh/pages/mag/> has a rich collection of resources and information about captioning.

- Captioning FAQ
  <http://main.wgbh.org/wgbh/pages/mag/services/captioning/faq/>
- Caption Services
  <http://main.wgbh.org/wgbh/pages/mag/services/captioning/>
- Media Access Group Guides include Vol. 7 The Educational Uses of Captioning
  <http://main.wgbh.org/wgbh/pages/mag/resources/guides/>
- WGBH Accessible Webcasts
  <http://main.wgbh.org/wgbh/access/accesswebcast.html>
- Information for parents and teachers
  <http://main.wgbh.org/wgbh/pages/mag/resources/info-parent-teachers.html>

The Media Access Group also provides the service know as *MoPix*, which is available in some movie theatres, to make feature films accessible to patrons who have visual and hearing impairments. A current listing of theatres in the United States and Canada that have installed Rear Window® Captioning and DVS Theatrical® technologies is available. To learn more about this service and find theatres in North America with this technology, visit the *MoPix* Web site <http://ncam.wgbh.org/mopix/>. This resource can be shared with colleagues who work with students who have visual and hearing impairments. It can help educators plan events and field trips including feature films that may be enjoyed by all students. The National Institute on Deafness and Other Communication Disorders (NIDCD) has an informative page that reviews various types of captioning formats and the legal obligations related to captioning <http://www.nidcd.nih.gov/health/hearing/caption.asp>. Links to captioning products and companies are listed on the Closed Captioning Web site <http://www.captions.org/softlinks .cfm>.

▶ Other Technologies

Developed at the National Technical Institute for the Deaf <http://ntidweb.rit.edu/>, C-Print is a computer speech-to-print transcription technology/service. It requires a note-taking assistant with an equipped laptop computer connected to another laptop or TV monitor where the text of the class lecture and discussions can be viewed. The note taker uses the computer to record the lecture and discussions, allowing the student with a hearing impairment to follow the text on the screen. Hard copies of the lecture and discussion notes can be printed for students in the class. Additional information about C-Print is available through the Northeast Technical Assistance Center (NETAC) Web site <http://www.netac.rit.edu/publication/tipsheet/ cprint.html> or <http://www.netac.rit.edu/downloads/TPSHT_ CPrint.pdf>.

Alternative products that do not require a student to work with a note taker or a sign language interpreter are available. iCommunicator software relies on speech-recognition technology to translate a speaker's voice into text and sign language on a portable laptop screen. The price of this sophisticated software is $3,999, and the software must be supported by a high-end laptop computer. Learn more about iCommunicator at the Interactive Solutions, Inc., Web site <http://www .myicommunicator.com>. Classroom Captioner™ from Personal Captioning Systems is over $7,000 for the computer, software, microphone, transmitter, and display system <http://www .personalcaptioning.com/cc.html>. These products may be options that are capable of providing some students with greater learning and communication independence. However, the speech-recognition technology that these systems use may result in speaker-recognition errors that could cause confusion and inaccurate translation. Trials of these expensive products and other forms of assistive technology should be carried out before considering a purchase.

NETAC has developed a series of very supportive teacher tip sheets on topics related to serving students with hearing impairments <http://www.netac.rit.edu/publication/tipsheet/>.

References

Captioning and Accessibility Information, Captioned Media Program, National Association of the Deaf <http://www.cfv.org/caai/ nadh23.pdf>.

Captioning Key: Guidelines and Preferred Techniques, Captioned Media Program, National Association of the Deaf <http://www.cfv.org/ caai/ nadh7.pdf>.

Davis, Cheryl, D., ***Demystifying Assistive Listening Devices***, WROCC Outreach Site at Western Oregon University Regional Resource Center on Deafness Western Oregon University, 1999 <http://www.wou.edu/education/sped/ nwoc/info.htm>.

Students with Hearing Disabilities, Houston Community College System <http://ccollege.hccs.cc.tx.us/instru/dssc/pdf/hearing.pdf>.

Chapter 13

Portable Technology Options

Students generally do not receive all of their education in one room. This is especially true in the upper grades where students routinely move from class to class as their schedules demand. Students are also unlikely to have unrestricted access to the library media center. Use may be restricted due to hours of operation, the access needs of other students and classrooms, and individual classroom teachers' instructional preferences and styles. Therefore, fixed assistive technology resources in the library media center offer limited learning support for students who are able to use the library when they need technology support.

Portable assistive technologies provide solutions for students who need technology support in more than one learning environment. Small, lightweight devices that arc casy to use and that can be carried from class to class can be a big help to students and their teachers. Library media specialists may consider the acquisition of portable assistive technologies to enhance resources and services. Library media specialists will want to consider the costs, functional value of devices, ease of implementation, sign-out procedures, policies, as well as device security issues. Some students with individual education plans may already have portable assistive technologies provided for them through special education services. It is important to consult with other staff to decide which portable devices would be most useful.

OCR Scanning and Text-Reading Devices

Handheld scanners with optical character recognition (OCR) software allow students who have difficulty taking notes to scan content from print material into a word processing document on a desktop or laptop computer. Reading pens are handheld scanners that convert scanned text to synthesized speech. These devices may be useful for students with reading disabilities. They can be used with an earphone in a library media center or classroom for reading support. Links to handheld scanners and reading pens are listed below:

- IRISPen II <http://www.irisusa.com>
- Reading Pen II, Quicktionary II, Quick Link Pen <http://www.wizcomtech.com>
- C-Pen <http://www.cpen.com>

Magnification Devices

Handheld magnifiers are available in a range of low- to high-tech options. Many office supply and variety stores carry plastic sheet magnifiers, magnifying lenses, and magnifying reading glasses. These products are less expensive than electronic handheld magnification devices such as portable CCTVs (closed circuit television systems). For a listing of portable CCTVs and links to vendor Web sites, visit the ABLEDATA searchable database and enter a keyword search for "CCTV" <http://www.abledata.com/Site_2/keyword.htm>. The ABLEDATA site also has a link to an online document, *Portable Video Magnifiers Fact Sheet*, that reviews the criteria for selecting a portable CCTV over other assistive options for people with visual impairments <http://www.abledata.com/text2/portmag.htm>.

Portable Keyboards

Many educators are using low-cost portable keyboards as an alternative to desktop and laptop computers. While these devices do not have the same computing potential as a high-powered computer, some portable keyboards come with built-in word processing, spreadsheet, typing tutor, word prediction, and add-on software options. Infrared text transfer capabilities allow users to "beam" selected text from their portable word processors to a printer, desktop, or laptop word processing software program where it can be stored, edited, and printed. This eliminates the need for students to use computer disks to transfer their work to another computer. Examples of popular low-cost portable keyboards are listed below:

- Laser PC-6 from Perfect Solutions
  <http://www.perfectsolutions.com>
- AlphaSmart 3000 and Dana from AlphaSmart
  <http://www.alphasmart.com>

Figure 13.1: Laser PC6 Portable Computer (nine built-in software programs and optional text-to-speech cartridge)
[Reprinted with permission from Perfect Solutions <http://www.perfectsolutions .com>.]

Cassette, CD, MP3 Players, and Other Devices

Portable cassette players are very inexpensive to purchase and are great for listening to books and other resources on tape. As well, many students have their own portable devices such as CD and MP3 players. CD and MP3 players can be used by students to access text with the use of software that converts text to WAV and MP3 files. Software such as *TextAloud MP3* from NextUp.com <http://www.nextup.com> and *Read and Write Gold* from textHELP! Systems Ltd. <http://www.texthelp.com> are capable of converting digital text to WAV and MP3 formats that students can listen to on their players. These products also include other literacy support features.

Personal digital assistants (PDAs) are handheld computers or pocket PCs with a growing number of software applications. These products have small display screens, which may make them less useful for users with visual impairments. However, educators are discovering that PDAs provide valuable support for students with cognitive and learning disabilities. Augmentative communication software is also available to help students with speech disabilities use their PDAs to speak for them. Information about PDA applications for people with disabilities is available online through the University of Toronto's Adaptive Technology Resource Centre <http://www.utoronto.ca/atrc/ reference/tech/pda.html>. Another excellent site developed by the University of Sussex Institute of Education's TechDis Accessibility

Database Team provides a well-organized overview of the value of PDAs for persons with disabilities <http://www.techdis.ac.uk/PDA/intro.htm>. Additional links to sources of pocket PC software can be found at PocketPCSoft.net <http://www.pocketpcsoft.net/> and HI-CE's Palm Pages <http://www.handheld.hice-dev.org/>.

Student Use Rules, Device Security, and Tracking Systems

Making portable assistive technology available to students in your school is one thing to consider, but keeping track of the devices that students are borrowing is another issue. It is appropriate to insist that students follow rules about handling the devices in order to retain the privilege of continuing to use them. Students requiring long-term portable technology support will likely have their technology needs met through special education technology service providers who have done a thorough assessment and assigned an appropriate device to the student for his or her personal use.

Library media centers that provide portable AT devices may find that there is a demand to use these tools from a wide range of students. Devices such as portable keyboards are convenient tools for many students. Products that appeal to a wide range of users will be in demand by many classes and students. Staff members will have to discuss whether class sets of portable computers should be available only for teacher sign out, or individual sign out as well.

If community groups also use the school and library media center when the staff is not on duty, device security becomes an important issue. Class sets of PDAs, portable CCTVs, reading pens, and other expensive devices must be locked up to discourage theft.

Devices that are signed out to individual teachers and students may also be lost, stolen, or damaged. Library media specialists can safeguard these resources by developing a checklist of user responsibilities to accompany the technology. Each person who signs out a device should read the checklist before the device is borrowed. Preventative measures will not eliminate all problems, but they will raise awareness about the value of the devices and the duty of care that is expected. Irresponsible use of the device should not be tolerated. Students must show a high level of responsibility in exchange for the privilege of using the resources.

Library media specialists can develop their own systems for tracking portable technology that is borrowed and returned. In a small library media center, a simple sign-up list may be all that is needed to keep tabs on AT devices and their users. In a large library media center, district center, or combined library and special education lending program, a more advanced system of tracking AT equipment use can be of value. Adaptive Solutions, Inc., has a software product called AT Tracker (Figure 13.2). This software can be used to record information about AT referrals, assessment, technical support, inventory, and checkout/check-in. AT Tracker also has reporting capabilities to help professionals evaluate their programs' activities and student AT needs. The 3M Company also has many library security products that may be suitable for tracking some AT devices. 3M provides some grants to school libraries for security systems <http://www.3m.com/market/security/library/>.

Figure 13.2: Assistive Technology Tracker [Reprinted with permission from Adaptive Solutions, Inc. <http://www.adaptive-sol.com>.]

▶ References

Providing Access to Portable Tools Collection, National Center to Improve Practice in Special Education Through Technology, Media and Materials <http://www2.edc.org/NCIP/library/laptops/toc.htm>.

Chapter 14

Creating Accessible Learning Materials

Computer technologies are making it easier for educators to create accessible learning materials for students. To ensure students have efficient access to existing Internet resources, educators should be aware of online eText resources and use these along with appropriate assistive technologies (see Appendix A—eText Resources). Sites with eText collections can be bookmarked or posted in a list near computers to encourage student use.

Educators interested in developing their own accessible books can make use of a variety of software programs. Additionally, students can be instructed on the use of multimedia authoring software to create accessible learning materials. Student-designed multimedia reading materials could be added to the library media center holdings where they would be available to others. As students hold copyright to their own work, educators should seek the permission of students and parents to use these materials. A variety of software programs have been used to develop accessible books, and some are mentioned later in this chapter. Some examples of accessible book collections are listed:

- SET-BC Accessible Books Project
  <http://www.setbc.org/resources/accbooks.html> or
  <ftp://ftp.setbc.org/pub/pdf02/acc_grid.pdf>
- Accessible Book Collection
  <http://www.accessibleBookcollection.org>
- Story Time Online
  <http://www.kennedy-center.org/multimedia/storytimeonline/>

- All Free Online Children's Books
  <http://www.allfreeonlinechildrensbooks.com>
- Award Winning Links
  <http://www.magickeys.com/books/links.html>

Resources

Talking photo albums are easy to assemble and can be used by students or staff to construct short talking books. An online article, *The Many Uses of Recordable Photo Albums* (Cormier, Carolann, MS, CCC-SLP, ATP) <http://www.connsensebulletin.com/books.html>, provides ideas about using talking photo frames and albums. The following are some available products:

- Talking Photo Album (24 pages)
  <http://www.liberator.co.uk/main.htm>
- Talking Photo Frames
  <http://www.radioshack.com/>

BookBuddi

BookBuddi is a shareware software product for Windows that can be downloaded and installed to create talking books and albums on the computer <http://bookbuddi1.tripod.com>. BookBuddi also requires the installation of the Microsoft Agent downloads Genie character and TruVoice text-to-speech engine <http://www.microsoft.com/msagent/downloads.htm>. Photos, images, and text can be copied into the pages, or text can be typed onto the BookBuddi page. The control panel allows the user to activate the text-to-speech software so the book can be read by a computer generated synthesized voice. BookBuddi is economical and easy to learn to use. See Figure 14.1.

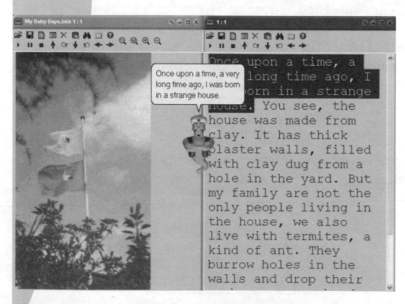

Figure 14.1: BookBuddi Screen Shot [Reprinted with permission from Paul B. Way <http://bookbuddi1.tripod.com>.]

Software is available that can help students who have organizational difficulties create graphic organizers, concept maps, and webs. Some of these products have hyperlink capabilities so that URLs typed onto the students' webs will link to specific Web pages on an Internet-connected computer. These products can be used to create Web quest templates or directories that simplify Internet research or help students to catalog important Internet resources. Some concept mapping software products are listed below:

- Inspiration and Kidspiration <http://www.inspiration.com>
- MindManager <http://www.mindjet.com>
- SoftNeuron Mindmap software <http://abonasoft.netfirms.com/softNeuronEn.html>
- SMART Ideas concept mapping software <http://www.smarttech.com>; it can be used on a computer and with the SMART Board Interactive Whiteboard

Fabula

Fabula is a multinational project funded by the European Commission. Fabula is a multimedia authoring project designed to allow school children and educators to author bilingual digital books. A paper about this project, *Fabula: A Bilingual Multimedia Authoring Environment for Children Exploring Minority Languages* (Edwards, V., et al, May 2002), is available online <http://llt.msu.edu/vol6num2/pdf/edwards.pdf). Visit the Fabula Web site <http://www.fabula.eu.org/> to learn more about this initiative and download free Fabula software. See Figure 14.2.

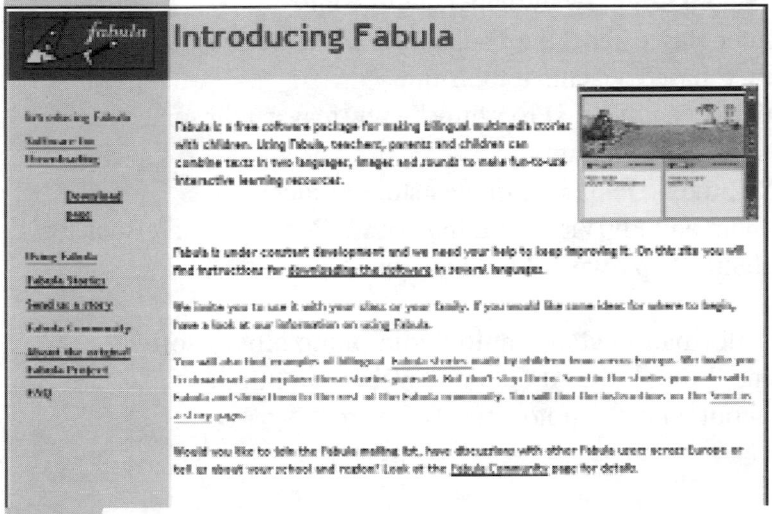

Figure 14.2: Fabula Project [Reprinted with permission from the Fabula Project <http://fabula.eu.org>.]

Creating Accessible Books Using PowerPoint, Clicker, and HyperStudio Software

Some excellent online booklets on how to use software programs to create accessible books are available through the Oxford ACE Centre <http://www.ace-centre.org.uk/> in the United Kingdom. The following guides authored by Richard Walter are part of this collection:

- *How to create Talking Books in PowerPoint*
- *How to create Talking Books in Clicker 4*
- *How to create Talking Books in HyperStudio 4*

The three guides are available as downloadable pdf files from the Oxford ACE Centre <http://www.ace-centre.org.uk/html/publications/publicat.html>.

Consult the list below for information about these and other software authoring products:

- BookBuddi <http://bookbuddi1.tripod.com>, shareware talking photo album or picture book reader
- PowerPoint <http://www.microsoft.com/office/powerpoint/>
- *Adding Narration to a PowerPoint Presentation* (Krauser, D.) and other tutorials <http://www.msdlt.k12.in.us/msdlt/StaffDevelopment/TechTutorials.html>
- Clicker <http://www.cricksoft.com/>
- HyperStudio <http://www.hyperstudio.com/>
- Computer-Based Teaching Tools <http://www.easyteach.com/computer_based_teaching_tools.htm>
- Speaking Dynamically Pro <http://www.mayer-johnson.com/software/Speakdyn.html>
- Kid Pix Studio Deluxe <http://teststore.broder.com/>
- FlipAlbum and FlipViewer <http://www.eBooksys.com/eBooksys/>
- 3D-Album <http://www.3d-album.com/>

More information about multimedia photo album software is reviewed online through the About.com Web site <http://graphicssoft.about.com/cs/photoalbumsoftware/>.

Copyright Laws (Reproduction for the Disabled)

Variable jurisdictional copyright laws must be considered when developing accessible books for students with disabilities. Information about current reproduction provisions for people with disabilities in American and Canadian copyright law is reviewed here.

Copyright Law of the United States (Chafee Amendment)

The **Chafee Amendment** (named after Rhode Island Republican Senator John Chafee) brought about permanent changes to the Copyright Law of the United States. On September 16, 1996, the bill became Public Law 104-197 when signed by President Clinton. This amendment means that the copyright permission process no longer applies in order for authorized entities to create specialized formats (Braille, audio, or digital text) for blind or other persons with disabilities eligible for specialized library services defined by the National Library Service for the blind and physically handicapped of the Library of Congress and its network of cooperating libraries. The Chafee Amendment is cited below:

Copyright Law of the United States
Chapter 1
Subject Matter and Scope of Copyright
§ 121. Limitations on exclusive rights: reproduction for blind or other people with disabilities

> *(a) Notwithstanding the provisions of section 106, it is not an infringement of copyright for an authorized entity to reproduce or to distribute copies or phonorecords of a previously published, nondramatic literary work if such copies or phonorecords are reproduced or distributed in specialized formats exclusively for use by blind or other persons with disabilities.*
>
> *(b)*
>
> > *(1) Copies or phonorecords to which this section applies shall—*
> > *(A) not be reproduced or distributed in a format other than a specialized format exclusively for use by blind or other persons with disabilities;*
> > *(B) bear a notice that any further reproduction or distribution in a format other than a specialized format is an infringement; and*
> > *(C) include a copyright notice identifying the copyright owner and the date of the original publication.*
> > *(2) The provisions of this subsection shall not apply to standardized, secure, or norm-referenced tests and related testing material, or to computer programs, except the portions thereof that are in conventional human language (including descriptions of pictorial works) and displayed to users in the ordinary course of*

using the computer programs.

(c) For purposes of this section, the term—

    (1) "authorized entity" means a nonprofit organization or a governmental agency that has a primary mission to provide specialized services relating to training, education, or adaptive reading or information access needs of blind or other persons with disabilities;

    (2) "blind or other persons with disabilities" means individuals who are eligible or who may qualify in accordance with the Act entitled "An Act to provide books for the adult blind", approved March 3, 1931 (2 U.S.C. 135a; 46 Stat. 1487) to receive books and other publications produced in specialized formats; and

    (3) "specialized formats" means braille, audio, or digital text which is exclusively for use by blind or other persons with disabilities.

[Chapter 1, Subject Matter and Scope of Copyright, § 121. Limitations on exclusive rights: reproduction for blind or other people with disabilities Copyright Law of the United States of America and Related Laws Contained in Title 17 of the United States Code Circular 92 <http://www.loc.gov/copyright/title17/92chap1.html>]

On January 29, 2003, a bill was introduced in the U.S. House of Representatives that may provide even more support for students with special needs in elementary and secondary schools in the United States. The ***Instructional Materials Accessibility Act of 2003*** is a bill that is designed to improve access to printed instructional materials used by blind or other persons with print disabilities in elementary and secondary schools, and for other purposes (H.R. 490, **Instructional Materials Accessibility Act of 2003** <http://thomas.loc.gov/cgi-bin/query/z?c108:H.R.490:>).

Section 8 of this bill outlines its relationship to the current provisions under Section 121 of the U.S. Copyright Act.

SEC. 8. RELATIONSHIP TO SECTION 121 OF THE COPYRIGHT ACT.

    (a) AUTHORIZED ENTITY—A publisher that provides instructional materials to a State educational agency or local educational agency in the national electronic file format prescribed under section 3(a), shall, for such purposes, be considered an authorized entity within the meaning of section 121 of title 17, United States Code.

> *(b) NONINFRINGING USE—Reproduction or distribution of instructional materials in a large print format exclusively for use by blind persons, or other persons with print disabilities, in elementary schools or secondary schools shall be considered a noninfringing use of such materials when conducted by an authorized entity (as that term is defined in section 121 of title 17, United States Code).*

Other sections of the U.S. Copyright Act also have an influence on the use of copyrighted materials in library media centers and classrooms:

- Section 107. Limitations on exclusive rights: Fair use <http://www.copyright.gov/title17/92chap1.html#107>
- Section 108. Limitations on exclusive rights: Reproduction by libraries and archives <http://www.copyright.gov/title17/92chap1.html#108>

The TEACH Act, which modifies Section 110 (2) of the U.S. Copyright Law, was signed into law by President George W. Bush on November 2, 2002. This legislation is important in addressing the use of copyrighted materials in the delivery of distance education. An online document and PowerPoint presentation review aspects of the TEACH Act and the duties and roles of instructors and librarians <http://www.ala.org/washoff/teach.html>.

Canadian Copyright Act [Section 32. (1)]

The *Council of Ministers of Education, Canada* has put together an online resource, ***Copyright Matters! Some Key Questions and Answers for Teachers***, that provides information about Canadian educational copyright issues. Answers to frequently asked questions are posted on the site along with links to other resources <http://www.cmec.ca/else/copyright/matters/indexe.stm>.

The Canadian Copyright Act is available online through the Government of Canada Web site <http://laws.justice.gc.ca/en/C-42/index.html>. Part III, [Section 32. (1)], *Persons with Perceptual Disabilities*, covers reproduction in alternate format as an exception to the infringement of copyright.

PART III
INFRINGEMENT OF COPYRIGHT AND MORAL RIGHTS AND EXCEPTIONS TO INFRINGEMENT
> *Persons with Perceptual Disabilities*
> *Reproduction in alternate format*
> *32. (1) It is not an infringement of copyright for a*

person, at the request of a person with a perceptual disability, or for a nonprofit organization acting for his or her benefit, to

> *(a) make a copy or sound recording of a literary, musical, artistic or dramatic work, other than a cinematographic work, in a format specially designed for persons with a perceptual disability;*
>
> *(b) translate, adapt or reproduce in sign language a literary or dramatic work, other than a cinematographic work, in a format specially designed for persons with a perceptual disability; or*
>
> *(c) perform in public a literary or dramatic work, other than a cinematographic work, in sign language, either live or in a format specially designed for persons with a perceptual disability.*

Limitation

(2) Subsection (1) does not authorize the making of a large print book.

Limitation

(3) Subsection (1) does not apply where the work or sound recording is commercially available in a format specially designed to meet the needs of any person referred to in that subsection, within the meaning of paragraph (a) of the definition "commercially available." R.S., 1985, c. C-42, s. 32; R.S., 1985, c. 10 (4th Supp.), s. 7; 1997, c. 24, s. 19.

Copyright Act, Chapter C-42, Department of Justice Canada <http://laws.justice.gc.ca/en/C-42/36488 .html#section-32>

The International Federation of Library Associations and Institutions has developed a very comprehensive listing of international links related to copyright issues <http://www.ifla.org/II/cpyright.htm>.

Copyright issues also relate to the use of proprietary software. It is important for educators purchasing assistive and educational software to understand their license agreements and responsibilities. Typically, schools purchase single-user, multiple-user, and site licenses. A single-user license is the least expensive option, but the software can only be installed on one computer (unless otherwise stated in the license agreement). Multiple-user licenses allow installation of the software on more than one computer. For example, a five-user license allows the software to be installed on five different computers. Site licenses allow the use of the purchased software on more computers throughout the facility (as stipulated in the license agreement). The Software and

Information Industry Association (SIIA) <http://www.siia.net> has developed a collection of resources related to software piracy and copyright issues. Information about software use and the law in the United States and Canada can be reviewed online through SIIA's anti-piracy link <http://www.siia.net/piracy/copyright/law.asp>.

In contrast to the copyright restrictions related to proprietary software, it is legal to copy, modify, distribute, and even sell software licensed under the GNU General Public License (GPL) <http://www.gnu.org/copyleft/gpl.html>. This includes existing and emerging GPLed Open Source assistive technologies—some of which have been displayed at leading assistive technology conferences. This is one of the aspects of Open Source software development that is so exciting, and why it has the potential to benefit so many (see Chapter 9 for more information on this topic).

References

Canadian Copyright Act, Department of Justice Canada <http://laws.justice.gc.ca/en/C-42/index.html>.

Canadian Guidelines on Library and Information Services for People with Disabilities, Canadian Library Association, February 1997 <http://www.cla.ca/about/disabils.htm>.

Copyright Law of the United States of America, Library of Congress <http://www.loc.gov/copyright/title17/92chap1.html>.

Cormier, Carolann, MS, CCC-SLP, ATP, *The Many Uses of Recordable Photo Albums* <http://www.connsensebulletin.com/books.html>.

Edwards, V., et al, Fabula: *A Bilingual Multimedia Authoring Environment for Children Exploring Minority Languages*, May 2002 <http://llt.msu.edu/vol6num2/pdf/edwards.pdf>.

GNU General Public License, Free Software Foundation, Inc., Boston, MA <http://www.gnu.org/copyleft/gpl.html>.

Chapter 15

Professional Development Resources for Educators

A lot of information has been presented in the previous chapters of this book to help readers learn about AT, but the dynamic nature of the field of assistive technology means that the learning is never really over. Innovative developments and upgrades will continue to bring new products, features, and greater opportunities within reach of people with disabilities. Professionals working in the AT field understand this and realize that networks of people and resources can help with the challenges of implementing innovative technologies. Joining or establishing a "mastermind" group of AT enthusiasts is one way of tapping into the collective intelligence of people around the world who share similar interests in using AT to help others.

If you are fortunate, you will have other professionals with knowledge of assistive technology in your school or district, who can offer advice and troubleshoot. Many districts in the United States have developed sophisticated services and support teams for inservice training, consultation, and student assessment. If you are professionally isolated in a jurisdiction that hasn't embraced assistive technology as an educational priority, it may be more of a challenge to advance yourself professionally and achieve your AT implementation goals. In this circumstance, you'll need to establish your own support network. Reaching out to like-minded professionals beyond your own district can be an exciting way to expand your horizons.

Online Training

Online training opportunities help educators learn more about AT and can accommodate a busy schedule better than college or university-based courses with rigid class times. There are free self-directed learning options, as well as advanced instructor led tuition-based online training courses, that lead to certificates or continuing education unit (CEU) credits. Some options are listed below:

- University at Buffalo Assistive Technology Training Online Project <http://atto.buffalo.edu/>
- Research Institute for Assistive and Training Technologies (RIATT) Professional Development Program <http://www.nasdse.com/>
- Virtual Assistive Technology University (University of Southern Maine) <http://www.vatu.usm.maine.edu/courses.htm>
- California State University, Northridge (CSUN) Assistive Technology Applications Certificate Program (ATACP) <http://www.csun.edu/codtraining/brochure/atacp/index2.htm>

Online Discussion and Collegial Support Groups

Some online training programs such as CSUN's ATACP have a companion discussion group (listserv) that participants can join to exchange information about assistive technology. However, it is not necessary to take a course in order to participate on Internet discussion groups. A number of e-groups have emerged since the mid 1990s to support professionals with an interest in assistive technology. Educators do not have to pay a fee to join these groups. Messages are archived with keyword search features that support topic research. Participants can ask questions, share information, or just review the messages posted by group members. Some active AT discussion groups are listed here:

- Assistive Technology Canada Listserv <http://ca.groups.yahoo.com/group/ATCanada/>
- AT-Group <http://groups.yahoo.com/group/AT-Group/>
- attechnology e-group <http://groups.yahoo.com/group/attechnology/>
- QIAT Listserv <http://sweb.uky.edu/~jszaba0/qiatlistserv.html>
- Other AT-related discussion groups and newsletters can be found through the Yahoo! Groups page <http://groups.yahoo.com>. Enter "assistive technology" or another term in the search box to find a discussion group that meets your needs.

- Closing the Gap Forums host free moderated AT/special needs discussions that usually continue for one or two weeks. The discussions are archived on the site so that information can be reviewed at any time <http://www.closingthegap.com>.

These groups give experienced and inexperienced participants the opportunity to connect and support one another through the AT learning process. Members with knowledge of specific technologies and students with unique learning needs exchange information and advice.

Professional Perspectives

Assistive technology specialists offer advice:

As an AT specialist, what recommendations would you give to library media specialists to assist them in creating an accessible library?

Gayl Bowser, M.S.
Gayl Bowser is the coordinator of the Oregon Technology Access Program (OTAP). She has received awards for her work as an educator and consultant in the fields of special education and assistive technology.

- Know the students with disabilities in your school and the tasks that they are required to do in your library. Talk to the students themselves as well as the professionals who work with them.
- Look for barriers in your library that would keep students with disabilities from completing those tasks.
- Make sure that you have not created barriers by placing racks too close or computers too high, or by using technology that cannot be adapted.
- Know the ways that your existing technology can be adapted to meet the needs of students who encounter access barriers. This would include simple accommodations, such as the use of a library aide to help a student get a book off a shelf, as well as high-tech accommodations, such as changes in the settings of the operating systems of your computers.
- Know who you can call upon for help if you need to have more information about eliminating barriers by using assistive technology for the students with disabilities in your school library.

Penny Reed, Ph.D.
Penny Reed is the founder and director of the Wisconsin Assistive Technology Initiative (WATI). She has worked as a teacher, a consultant, and an administrator in Oregon and Wisconsin for over 30 years.

■ Think about making the physical library and the library materials accessible to all of the following:
  • Students with mobility problems who need wide aisles and room to navigate.
  • Students who are seated in wheelchairs and may not be able to see or reach items on high shelves.
  • Students who cannot understand verbal directions and need print combined with picture symbols to know what is expected of them.
  • Students who are emergent readers and need a large variety of books at their reading level or adapted for their reading level.
  • Students who understand at their grade level but read several grades lower and may need to have materials scanned and spoken by a computer.
  • Students who could understand material from the Internet, but need it read loud.
  • Students who might need help only with a few difficult words and could use a small handheld speaking scanner.
■ Watch students and see what frustrates them. Try to follow up and find out what they need. It may already be there, but they may not be able to find it.
■ Make sure teachers, student helpers, and others know what AT tools you have available, how to access them and how to use them.
■ Ensure that the AT is working and ready to use so that users don't become frustrated.
■ Become familiar with several key Web sites that will keep you current on AT and its uses.

Associations and Organizations

Memberships in professional associations and organizations can help agencies, institutions, and educators become connected to others with similar interests in assistive technology services.

■ Alliance for Technology Access <http://www.ataccess.org/>
■ Assistive Technology Industry Association <http://www.atia.org/>

- Association for the Advancement of Assistive Technology in Europe <http://www.fernuni-hagen.de/FTB/AAATE.html>
- Council for Exceptional Children <http://www.cec.sped.org/>
- Rehabilitation Engineering and Assistive Technology Society of North America (RESNA) <http://www.resna.org/>

Certification Programs

Increasingly, colleges and universities in the United States are offering certificate courses in assistive technology. These programs can range from approximately 15 hours of course work to several months to complete. Check with postsecondary institutions nearest to you to find out if programs are available in your region.

Options that require more independent work experience or study are available. The CSUN ATACP mentioned earlier requires online module completion as well as some classroom instruction and a project. People who take the CSUN program must be willing to travel to one of the classroom instructional sites to complete the requirements of the course.

RESNA offers several assistive technology credentialing options that require candidates to pass a written exam. However, specific employment and educational requirements must be met before candidates are eligible to write the RESNA exams. RESNA exams are scheduled throughout the year in different cities in North America. Candidates must travel to one of these exam sites to write the test.

A selection of online AT competency certificates is available through the National Association of State Directors of Special Education (NASDSE). These include a *Basic Competency Certificate*, an *Educators Competency Certificate*, and an *Administrators Competency Certificate*. More information is available online <http://www.nasdse.com/competency_certificates.html>.

EASI (Equal Access to Software and Information) has initiated a series of online courses that can lead to an EASI Certificate in Accessible Information Technology and continuing education credits <http://easi.cc/workshop.htm>. Courses available through EASI now include lesson content about accessible library IT [*Barrier-free Information Technology Syllabus* <http://easi.cc/workshops/adaptit.htm>].

According to EASI CEO, Norm Coombs, Ph.D., EASI has integrated the library lesson into other lessons and no longer has a special lesson. "We have worked closely with ALA (American Library Association) over the years and many librarians have taken all of our courses, especially the Web accessibility courses. We have a listserv for librarians. Send e-mail to <*listserv@maelstrom.stjohns.edu*> saying *sub axslib-l* (and include your name). It is now the only Internet discussion list dedicated to library access issues." In 2000, the Association of Specialized and Cooperative Library Agencies (ASCLA) presented Coombs with the Francis Joseph Campbell Award of the American Library Association for his work on accessibility.

▶ Conferences

Conferences on assistive technology offer participants the opportunity to attend a wide range of educational sessions on technologies, policy, disability-specific issues, and many AT-related topics. While some major national and international conferences have been taking place for the last 15 to 20 years, there are more recently initiated regional conferences and seminars being offered by school districts and other organizations. The major conferences can be expensive to attend if you have to travel long distances, but the selection of educational topics and the variety of technologies on display present valuable learning opportunities for educators and others.

The following conferences provide an impressive selection of educational presentations, AT demonstrations, and exhibits.

- The Assistive Technology Industry Association (ATIA) Conference is held annually in January in Florida <http://www.atia.org/>.
- The California State University, Northridge (CSUN) Technology and Persons with Disabilities Conference is held annually in March in Los Angeles, California <http://www.csun.edu/cod/>.
- The Closing the Gap Conference is held annually in October in Minneapolis, Minnesota <http://www.closingthegap.com/>.

These conferences attract thousands of participants every year. Other assistive technology conferences held throughout the world can be found through the *Calendar of Events in Disability, Rehabilitation, and Assistive Technology* <http://www.starlingweb.com/adp/as00024e .htm>. RehabTool.com also has a very good online calendar of assistive technology events and training <http://www.rehabtool.com/events .html#2>.

Library media specialists can become well-informed partners in the delivery of assistive technology services to students with disabilities. The assistive technology conferences that have been mentioned attract a wide range of educators, consumers, and other professionals. The large conferences such as CSUN, ATIA, and Closing the Gap include many sessions and exhibits that would be helpful to library media specialists.

Regional and national library conferences that are already educating library media specialists about current issues and resources could be further enriched through the addition of exhibits and educational sessions that focus on assistive technology options for the library media center. The introduction of an assistive technology component to an established library conference could add an innovative dimension to a regularly scheduled event. Assistive technology resellers, developers, and specialists could provide educational sessions and exhibits that demonstrate products appropriate for K–12 library media center use.

Library media specialists and other educators have the opportunity to build collaborative AT-related networks through Internet discussion groups, conferences, and new professional events and associations. There's never been a better time to connect with colleagues on a global scale and collectively work toward the development of technology enhanced learning opportunities that will benefit all students.

▶ Australian Study

Dr. Janet Murray has extensive library management experience in local government, state government, schools, and colleges of further education in both Australia and the United Kingdom. She has been a lecturer in management, information management, and librarianship at the University of Melbourne, RMIT University, and the University of Ballarat in Australia. Her doctoral research examined the provision of services to school students with special needs. Murray now works as a trainer and management consultant across a range of sectors including the education, library, and disability sectors. Past clients include the National Library of Australia, the State Library of Victoria, the Overseas Projects Corporation of Victoria, and the Victorian Electoral Commission.

Murray discusses the four-year Australian study she completed in 2000. This study evaluated aspects of school library provision for disabled students enrolled in mainstream schools.

"Data was collected by surveys and through interviews and observation in case study schools in Victoria and New South Wales, and focused on: the effectiveness of the special education model in the school, in terms of facilitating use by students with disabilities; awareness of disability legislation and its implications for library services; library staff's personal experience of disability, or relevant staff development programs; standard of physical access to the library; the range of alternative format materials available, and knowledge of outside sources where they could be obtained; the range of special facilities (such as adaptive technology) available in the library for students with disabilities; and the teaching of information skills. The study also focused on the relationship between the library staff and the special education staff, and the effect this had on school library provision and the acquisition of information skills by students with disabilities.

"The study found that the culture of the school and its implications for management and communication was an important factor in the success of the library program for students with disabilities. Well-established, two-way communication between the library staff and the special education staff and a good relationship between the school librarian and the principal were critical factors. These elements could be affected by the size of the school. Personal experience of disability, or experience of disability awareness training, on the part of library staff [members] meant that they did not feel uneasy in dealing with students with disabilities and more readily understood their needs. Involvement of special education staff in the design of information skills programs, and the support of aides where necessary for students using the library, enabled effective information skills programs to be offered to students with disabilities. There was however a low level of provision of alternative format materials and adaptive technology in the majority of school libraries.

"An interesting development that could impact on this area is the creation of learning support centers in some schools. These involve administrative amalgamation of special education, information technology support, and school library services. Computers, software, books, curriculum materials, and teaching resources are available in one location alongside personnel who can provide learning support, technology support and expertise on resources. If this trend continues, it would seem to offer the ideal environment for school librarians to further enhance services for students with disabilities."

References

Murray, Janet, "The Implications of Inclusive Schooling for School Libraries." *International Journal of Disability, Development & Education 49* (3), 2002, p.301–322.

Murray, Janet R., *The Response of School Libraries to the Inclusion of Students with Disabilities in Mainstream Schools*. Ph.D. Thesis (Monash University) 2000.

Murray, Janet, "School Libraries ... Enabling the Disabled through Adaptive Technology." *Access* **14 (4)** 2000, p.20–23.

Murray, Janet, "Teaching Information Skills to Students with Disabilities: What Works?" *School Libraries Worldwide*, 7 (2), July 2001, 1–16.

▶ Appendix A

Free eText Resources

- Alex Catalogue of Electronic Texts
  <http://www.infomotions.com/alex/>

- American Memory: Historical Collections for the National Digital Library <http://memory.loc.gov/>

- Arthur's Classic Novels
  <http://www.unityspot.com/arthurs/index.html>

- Awesome Library—Literature
  <http://www.awesomelibrary.org/Classroom/English/Literature/Literature.html>

- Baen Free Library <http://www.baen.com/library/>

- Bartelby.com <http://www.bartleby.com/>

- Bibliomania <http://www.bibliomania.com>

- Books-Online.com <http://www.books-online.com>

- CAST eText Spider <http://www.cast.org/udl/index.cfm?i=1300)

- ClassicAuthors.net <http://www.underthesun.cc/Classics/>

- Electronic Text Center, Cornell University
  <http://www.library.cornell.edu/okuref/cet/cet.html>

- eServer.org <http://eserver.org/>

- eText Resources <http://www.textual.net/>

- Full Text Electronic Resources <http://www.star-host.com/library/eText.htm>

- KidPub.org <http://www.kidpub.org/kidpub/>

- LD Resources
  <http://www.ldresources.com/resources/eText/index.html>

- Literature.org <http://www.literature.org>

- PinkMonkey.com <http://www.pinkmonkey.com/>

- Project Gutenberg <http://www.gutenberg.org/>
  <http://www.promo.net/pg/list.html>

- SparkNotes Study Guides <http://www.sparknotes.com/>

- The Children's Literature Web Guide
  <http://www.acs.ucalgary.ca/~dkbrown/>

- The Internet Public Library <http://www.ipl.org/>

- The Online Books Page <http://digital.library.upenn.edu/books/>
- Traditional Stories Online Text
  <http://falcon.jmu.edu/~ramseyil/tradelec.htm>
- University of Texas Library Online
  <http://www.lib.utexas.edu/books/eText.html>
- University of Virginia Library Electronic Text Center
  <http://eText.lib.virginia.edu/english.html>

▶ Index